TRUST YOUR INTUITION

100 WAYS TO TRANSFORM
ANXIETY AND DEPRESSION
FOR STRONGER MENTAL HEALTH

JILL SYLVESTER, LMHC

OLD TREE HOUSE
PUBLISHING

TRUST YOUR INTUITION
100 Ways to Transform Anxiety and Depression for Stronger Mental Health
BY JILL SYLVESTER, LMHC

Old Tree House Publishing

Published by Old Tree House Publishing Hanover, MA
Copyright ©2019 Jill Sylvester
All rights reserved.

No part of this publication may be reproduced, stored in a retrieval system, or transmitted in any form or by any means, electronic, mechanical, photocopying, recording, scanning, or otherwise, except as permitted under Section 107 or 108 of the 1976 United States Copyright Act, without the prior written permission of the Publisher. Requests to the Publisher for permission should be addressed to Permissions Department, Old Tree House Publishing, PO Box 462, Hanover, MA 02339

Limit of Liability/Disclaimer of Warranty: While the publisher and author have used their best efforts in preparing this book, they make no representations or warranties with respect to the accuracy or completeness of the contents of this book and specifically disclaim any implied warranties of merchantability or fitness for a particular purpose. No warranty may be created or extended by sales representatives or written sales materials. Neither the publisher nor author shall be liable for any damages arising here from. The strategies contained herein may not be suitable for every situation.

The material in this book is not intended to provide any type of psychological counseling. If you feel you need psychological counseling, seek the help of a qualified professional.

Editor: Lisa Tener | www.lisatener.com
Copyeditor: Jody Amato | jodyamato@gmail.com
Index: Elena Gwynne | www.quillandinkindexing.com
Cover and Interior design: Yvonne Parks | www.pearcreative.ca
Cover copy: Lisa Canfield | www.gethipcreative.com

Library of Congress Control Number: 2019939552

Publisher's Cataloging-In-Publication Data
(Prepared by The Donohue Group, Inc.)

Names: Sylvester, Jill, author.
Title: Trust your intuition : 100 ways to transform anxiety and depression for stronger mental health / Jill Sylvester, LMHC.
Description: Hanover, MA : Old Tree House Publishing, [2019] | Includes index.
Identifiers: ISBN 9780998977560 (paperback) | ISBN 9780998977577 (Kindle) | ISBN 9780998977584 (ePub)
Subjects: LCSH: Anxiety. | Depression, Mental. | Intuition. | Mental health. | Emotions. | Self-help techniques.
Classification: LCC BF575.A6 S95 2019 (print) | LCC BF575.A6 (ebook) | DDC 152.46--dc23

DEDICATION

To my clients past and present, who through the years, have come to trust their own inner navigation system. Witnessing you move from one space into another is the greatest reward of my work. This book is for you.

TABLE OF CONTENTS

PART II. TAKE GOOD CARE OF YOURSELF   **53**

PART III. BELIEVE   **87**

PART IV. TRUST YOUR INTUITION   123

PART V. FEEL BETTER — 161

INTRODUCTION

Deciding, truly deciding, that you want to raise the bar for your life is the most important step you can take in dealing with your depressed and anxious feelings. You are not the label of depression and anxiety, those heavy words we often assign to ourselves that tend to keep us stuck on that rigid plane. These are feelings we can do something about. The moment you separate from that lower vibration and decide you truly want something different for yourself—not just in theory, but in action—you change your story. Just as important as noticing what you don't want is deciding what you do want. Congratulate yourself for wanting to become unstuck; that declaration alone is what prompts change.

The following pages offer 100 tips and techniques that I use with clients in my private practice as a licensed mental health counselor with a holistic and alternative bent. My clients include adults, adolescents, children, and parents.

But I wasn't always a therapist.

Before that, I worked in the corporate world in management, my identity for many years, until I had my first child. Then, suddenly awakening to my intuition, which rocked my world, my priorities changed. And before that? I was a college student, struggling deeply with anxiety and depression, suffering actually—I always had, all the way back to when I can first remember. I didn't know any differently. That's just the way it was—and how I thought it was always going to be.

This book includes the tools I have used in my own personal development over a period of almost thirty years. I know that these techniques work. I live them. When we apply the tools on a regular basis—not just when we feel like doing them, or when depression and anxiety rear their dark energy—and work our own personal programs and become consistent in our self-care, we see results. I have found, both in my own life and in the lives of my clients, that unlocking your own intuition is the key to change. Good mental health is *everything*. It affects our relationships, our jobs, our role as parents, our selves as we seek our purpose. The only way out of those difficult feelings is to make the choice to move through those feelings—to learn more about yourself in the process, coming to understand that when you do the work, you become better able to serve. And that's really, I believe, the point for us all.

Take your time with each section. Perhaps simply focus on just one technique each day. When you're ready, move forward. Use the Call to Action PART included with each technique as you wish—if you are a writer, choose a journal or notebook to record your feelings. If you are an artist, doodle your reflections through color and imagery. If you are a thinker, then simply ponder the questions in a hot bath, on a morning run, or in your car on a long drive, letting your mind bring you to the answers that serve you best. The important thing is to apply what you learn. Knowledge holds power, but wisdom is rooted in application.

Lastly, why did I choose the word *transform* in the title when I could have used *overcome*, as I did originally? First, I had a dream that there was a better word. Second, when I looked up the definition of transform, *Webster's New Dictionary* read: *to change the form or appearance of; to change the condition, nature, or function of.* That's exactly what you're going to achieve by reading and applying the techniques in this book. You're going to change the very nature of your anxiety and depression, by coming to understand the intuitive message behind both.

Enjoy the road ahead. I promise you, life gets better when you learn to trust your intuition. I'm grateful for learning to listen to mine, every day.

Thank you for reading,

Jill

PART I

HOLD ON

1

NAME YOUR FEELINGS

We're talking kindergarten stuff. Basic words—I'm sad, I'm frustrated, I'm happy—or like the artwork I have in my office drawer, written and illustrated by dozens of fantastic, spirited kids: I'm disappointed, I'm mad, I'm "super-dooper" happy. Feelings are raw emotions. One-word adjectives. Many people struggle with identifying their basic feelings and giving them a voice. When you can get to the feeling, you can get to the root emotion—not just the word, but the imprint, the energy that goes along with the feeling. When you embrace your true feelings, that's when the tears come, and when the shift toward wellness begins. By naming your feelings, you release that previously blocked energy, which holds you back from peace, lightness, and moving forward. Emotional awareness is key. Practice naming your feelings every day. When you feel happy, say so. Acknowledge your happiness. When you feel mad, say you're mad, out loud. Get used to identifying the way you feel. This one action step will help you gain more power over feelings of anxiety and depression.

Call To Action

What do you feel right now? What did you feel this morning? This afternoon? Yesterday? How many feelings are you feeling right now? Do you know what your loved ones are feeling right now? Ask them and begin having conversations of substance in order to communicate about what counts and to understand one another better. Notice how you feel as a result.

2

WHEN YOU FEEL PANICKED, HOLD ON (LITERALLY)

As Harriet Lerner, Ph.D., so eloquently states in *Fear and Other Uninvited Guests*, "If you are alive, you have an anxiety disorder." We have all experienced anxiety and its crippling energy. When the wave hits—you know the feeling, the one that threatens to take you under—hold on to a desk or the sides of your chair; squeeze your hands together; grip a pen, something, anything, to anchor yourself until the wave passes. It will. The feeling always subsides. Holding on to something tangible allows you to feel the feeling—yes, feel it, in all its intensity—knowing and trusting that you're going to come through, that your heart rate will decrease, and that *you will be okay.*

The physical act of holding helps to tether you through the big, huge shaky feelings, anchoring your experience, pulling you from a ten on the panic scale down to perhaps a five, where the feeling becomes more manageable. Be conscious of your emotions. Allow them to come, allow them to go—not running or escaping the awfulness because of the pain. Then, and only then, can you consider the next best move.

Some of my greatest insights and revelations have occurred by allowing the fear to come, akin to sitting in a flimsy house in the midst of a tornado. It's a brutal experience when it's happening, I know, but I believe anxiety is never meant to torture us, even though it feels that way. Anxiety serves to strengthen us, so we can arrive on the other side, knowing we made it through, safe and stronger because of our choice to be brave and to feel the feelings. (Sometimes, I've discovered, anxiety deepens our intuition, as we who get anxious are highly sensitive to our feelings.) Anxiety is how the body sends us messages that capture our attention, alerting us to the trigger thought or situation that preceded the anxious feeling. (More on coming to know and understand your triggers later.)

Call to Action:

When was the last time you felt high anxiety? How did you feel when it was over? If you held on, what could you hold onto? Would you be willing to allow the feeling to come the next time, and perhaps see what the anxiety has to say? How do you think you would feel when it was over? Stand in that feeling. Make note of your impressions. Decide you want more of that feeling.

FEELING STUCK? PHYSICALLY MOVE OUT OF THE SPACE YOU'RE IN

This tool is great for those who may struggle with Obsessive-Compulsive Disorder (OCD). Here's how the exercise works: When you find yourself engaged in thought patterns that have you stuck in negative emotions, get up and move. Literally, stand up and move out of the space. In *The Brain That Changes Itself,* Norman Doidge,

M.D., writes with regard to OCD, "It is essential to *do* something, to 'shift' the gear manually."

When you find yourself doing things you don't want to be doing, or in conversations you don't want to be having, move to the left, the right, forward, backward. Change up the energy, even if you have no idea what you're going to do in the next moment. Anything is better than being stuck in a negative space.

Picture yourself standing in a cloud of grey fog, which is how I visualize depression. When you move out of the fog, you're no longer in the fog. You may feel as if you are being held hostage in that prison-like, grey space, or stuck behind that intimidating wall, but when you become aware, you realize you are free to move and that you have a choice. Yes. You do. Choice is one of the greatest tools already available to you in your tool bag.

Call to Action:

What's a space you often find yourself in that no longer makes you feel good? What are you willing to do physically the next time you find yourself standing in that space? How would you feel if you moved out of that foggy, grey space into a clearer one? What might that do for your future when you no longer choose to participate in the chaos? What if what lies on the other side is infinitely better than what you can imagine for yourself today? What are you waiting for?

4

STATE OUT LOUD: "WE'RE NOT DOING THAT ANYMORE"

This has become one of my recent favorite techniques for change. Positive, declarative statements help defeat self-destructive patterns by reprogramming your thoughts.

Clap your hands for emphasis while you say out loud, "We're not doing that anymore." When you choose this action, you send a message to your brain that you're no longer willing to do the same thing you have done time and time again with the same self-destructive, maladaptive results.

By stating an opposing thought to the negative behavior, you create a space to open to something new— even if you don't know what to do just yet. The possibilities will present themselves in ways they hadn't before when you were engaging in familiar behavior patterns. When you challenge your anxious and depressed symptoms in this manner, you emerge feeling empowered, which prompts entirely new options for your life.

Call to Action

What patterns and behaviors do you have in your life that you'd like to change? What would it look like if you were to decide you weren't going to take part in that behavior anymore? When you are willing to state out loud, "We're not doing that anymore," how might you feel? Do this exercise the next time you want to change your behavior. Note how you feel after you make the choice.

TIGHTEN AND RELEASE

This technique, which I typically use with anxious children, helps release excess feelings inside the body and can also benefit adults. The exercise dispels nervous feelings, overwhelm, and also functions to release the energy buildup from the day. Here's how it works: Squeeze everything tight—your face, hands, feet and core, tight, tighter, and then release. Visualize tension leaving your body, tension you may not have even realized existed. Rate the tension, or anxious feelings, on a scale of 1-10, and then compare how you feel after you go through the exercise a minimum of three to seven times. You might find the technique takes the anxiety only down from a nine to a five. That's okay. You don't need to eradicate anxiety to a zero or even one. You simply want to lessen the intensity of the feeling in order to hold the feeling in your hands, so to speak, so that it becomes workable and within your control. I used this technique nightly with my own children as the last thing they did before going to bed. Like squeezing out a sponge filled with excess, you let go of what you no longer need.

Call to Action

List three things that felt stressful to you today and that you'd like to release. Consciously choose to let go of each stressor as you exhale, reducing stress and inflammation, allowing your body to clear and to feel peace. Choose this tool the next time you feel anxious and note how you feel.

6

GROUND YOURSELF

One of the hardest feelings, in my opinion, is overwhelm. When your anxious thoughts feel like they're getting to be too much, immediately press your feet into the Earth, whether that means the floor beneath you or outside on the grass. When we feel anxious, we feel out of our bodies, because energetically we are. Have you ever noticed that when you feel confident and self-assured, you feel solid, rooted in your lower half? Grounding exercises redistribute that dizzying energy in your head back down into your legs.

When you choose to use a grounding tool, you make a conscious decision to feel better. Try exercise, including yoga or qigong. Walk or run outside, feeling nature around you and beneath your feet. Twist in place, bringing the energy down from your head and into the rest of your body. Walk outside barefoot, feeling the negative ions in the Earth. Food can also ground; good, earthy, dense food that brings you comfort. In order to feel secure, you need to feel connected to the Earth.

Call to Action

When do you feel grounded? What are you willing to do to ground yourself the next time you feel anxious? What are you willing to do every day to proactively ground yourself in order to feel stable and secure? Incorporate this practice into your daily routine. Once you make a decision to feel better, watch how your thoughts begin to guide you in a more positive direction.

7

DIVE DOWN INTO YOUR DEPRESSION

What I've realized about depression is that when you choose to be brave enough to step inside depression's wide-eating jaws to see what the beast might have to offer, you emerge stronger as a result of the risk. Caution: This is scary as shit. However, if you really want to grow and are committed to more powerful mental health, you'll do this, by choice.

When depressive feelings show up, making you feel like you're walking through waist-high sand, know that these feelings show up for a reason. Your job becomes searching for the jewel in the wreckage. Give your depression a voice, a name, an external energy with the intention of consciously confronting the obstacle blocking your path. By choosing to face that energy and diving deep, you shed yet another layer of the fear-based exterior you have created for yourself, bringing you closer to who you really are.

Align with that obstacle energy in order to make a change, altering your perspective of depression and taking advantage of the opportunity it offers. Depression can right your course, reminding you when you veer off a healthier, more meaningful path. Here's the thing about allying with depressive-type feelings: the more you listen to and join forces with that energy, the quicker you exit the darkness.

I swear.

When you start to sense you're slipping into that frightening black space, that feeling like you're most certainly going to be swallowed whole, grab your journal if it's nearby, or talk out loud in your car, asking, "Okay darkness, okay shark-like beast, what do I need to know?"

The alternative is remaining stuck in the previous pattern of having depression hang around too long, maybe for years, never having received the message it brings. By that time, people are often hospitalized. Been there.

Be brave. Choose to move through that shadowy, looming wall. You must know the contrast of darkness before you can recognize and revel in the light.

PERSONAL SHARE

Having come from a long lineage of depressed people (no hard feelings, family members past and present; our DNA has made me a better therapist), the "depressing" feelings I sometimes experience today differ vastly from the depression of my youth. When depression-type feelings arise for me in my present life, I find the feelings far more constructive and purposeful.

Let me give you an example of a recent time I felt "depressed" (I put the word in quotation marks because that's how the word has come to feel to me: symptoms of standard depression, yes, but this time around, I know better than to buy into the totality of that clinical, fear-based message). A few years ago, one August, I felt particularly blue—like I was screaming inside myself but no words would come out. For a period of almost forty-eight hours, I slowed down as if in slow motion, my vibration nearly coming to a halt, the last night of which I became almost entirely catatonic.

I didn't know what was happening or why. I remember sitting at my son's baseball game, directly in front of my neighbor, who also happens to be a good friend. I couldn't turn around to talk to her. I truly couldn't move, other than to get to the car and back. It was like I was one hundred years old, moving with only the minimal energy I could muster. I also didn't eat for two days. (If you know me, I love, and live, to eat). I felt stuck big time. If you've never experienced depressed symptoms like this, I'm thrilled for you. If you have, you know exactly what I mean. While the feelings were so intense that I could definitely have been considered hospital material, I still knew, in that intuitive way that requires no explanation to anyone else, that I'd be okay.

Having been down this road before, after I began my own deep psychological work years ago, I sat with the "depression" as soon as I had the chance to go within. I didn't run from the darkness. I dove down deep. Meaning, I sat as still as possible in a space of solitude, giving my depression the permission to enter my space. Then, I waited for answers. I did this daily, with a clear, specific intention. *What do you want me to know?*

Little moments of clarity would come: things like needing to take more days off, being perhaps a little burnt out from the busy counseling schedule I kept. I loved my work; I knew that wasn't the entire answer. Movement of energy stirred in my mind, my intuition speaking louder, rising closer to the surface as I sat in stillness. More flickers of clarity. Yes, there was definitely more information making its way to me. Something was missing from my life. I waited once again. Then, after a period of a few days, I struck gold. I realized I needed to get back to my first love: writing.

I'd always been a writer; it's been my dream since I could hold a pen in my hand. *If I could ever get to it, I could learn how to take my passion and develop that love into a skill.* Yes, the writing again. After that knowing, specific messages started to arrive in greater amounts. Fiction. *I loved children's books most.* That had been my greatest desire. I loved being a therapist and, of course, a wife and mother. But there was more to me, more for me to do. Two months later, with ideas flowing like rain, I started writing my first young adult novel, *The Land of Blue.* If I hadn't listened and joined forces with my "depression," I wonder if I would have accomplished writing the novel that has become my heart and soul.

Call to Action

Where do you feel stuck? Notice your feelings around this dark energy. Listen closely. What does your "depression" say to you? Write down your ideas. Like a magician who pulls the never-ending scarf out of his mouth, keep writing, keep crying, keep expressing until you have nothing left. Then see what remains.

8

DON'T LISTEN TO YOUR GREMLINS

When your thoughts tell you that you are less than, that life isn't fair, that you're not good-looking enough, smart enough, funny enough, social enough—you get the underlying vibe—understand this is the sneaky, strategic work of your gremlins. A tactic of your lower self to keep you down, to keep you stuck behind that grey wall. Your gremlins want to prevent you from moving forward toward your destiny. When you come to discern the voice of your sneaky self (which sounds similar to the passive-aggressive or straight-up aggressive people in your life) it becomes far easier to state the following declarative sentence, in your mind, or out loud if you're home alone, "Quiet down, m*****f****r."

Once you establish the upper hand, the energy moves out more quickly each time. Gremlins never really go away, BTW—you always have a lower self to address. The gremlins simply become easier to outsmart. One of the greatest parts of my job is observing clients growing stronger in their backtalk. I find the process similar to watching a flower bloom over time. Simply beautiful. Talk back to your gremlins the nanosecond you hear their negative voices. Your job becomes recognizing their mal-intention. Your highest self, your angels, your guides, your wise mind, would never speak to you that way. You decide which voice you want to listen to.

Call to Action

How do your gremlins speak to you? What do they say? If you could imagine your gremlins sitting in front of you, what would they look like? What do they hold you back from? When do they show up? Are you okay with that? What is something you could say to your gremlins the next time they whisper in your ear or slam the cymbals inside your brain? Decide and then make this one of your repeated mantras and watch what happens over the course of a few months. Be consistent with your efforts. Enjoy the results.

PRACTICE MEDITATION

This technique's a game-changer and a top practice to combat anxious feelings and overall depression. My clients who eventually come around to meditation have incredible results. Meditation allows a space all your own—with God, the Universe, whatever you believe— to consciously breathe life into your energy field. There are so many apps and guided meditations to choose from, but the basic premise of meditation is learning to sit, to breathe, and to relax.

You can do this anywhere: in your car, at your desk, or in bed. Breathe in deeply and intentionally. Exhale what you don't want in your body. Breathe in for a count of three and out for a count of four. Or try this other breathing method I've used for years—Dr. Andrew Weil's technique of breathing in for four, holding for seven, and breathing out for eight. I add visualization: breathing in golden healing light for four, distributing that healing energy from head to toe, in and around every cell in your body for a count of seven, and then exhaling, picturing car exhaust fumes leaving your body for a count of eight. Long, intentional, purposeful breathing during each exhale dispels what your body does not need. This technique has helped me stay healthy and clear for all the years I've used it.

Breathing is the first part of meditation. Then you simply hold the space. You might listen to a guided meditation, someone's voice you respect, or to sounds of the ocean, thunder, or rain. Whatever feels right for you is the method you choose. Tomorrow your meditation might be something different. Here's the thing: you don't have to sit and wait for the screen to clear and your mind to become blank in order to be a true meditator; that's not what I believe, anyway. If you are going for that, great, but I think that's what scares most people— that they aren't doing things right. That pressure might cause you to feel agitated and upset, which can be a deal breaker.

Here's another tip: Make your meditation a visualization practice. Breathe in first, preparing yourself for calmness, the same way you'd optimally want to feel before driving your car. Then focus on the things you want to have, the feelings you want to feel, the person you want to become. Breathe life into that mental picture. That can be your meditation, too. Begin where you are. Build your practice from there.

PERSONAL SHARE

Most mornings, I do the four-seven-eight breathing technique for a few rotations, starting the day by gathering the energy I need. I visualize my day and how I want things to go, like a gentle, meandering road, ending with my head on the pillow each night, feeling like I've done the best I could with the tools I have. Being a person who works with energy, I make sure my own field starts the day cocooned in strong, powerful light. My kids and I used to call this "putting your bubble around you" when they were little, which means protecting yourself and establishing boundaries so that you know who you are, what you stand for, and are not so easily influenced or affected by others.

After I visualize my energetic field as strong and secure, I send light to my family members, their schools, cars, our home, our friends, neighbors, our town, my clients, my people, onto our country and then the world. I do this every morning. Meditation takes just a few minutes. The practice is well worth your time, for this sacred twenty-four hours sets up your tomorrow and the days after that. Today is your future. Meditating each morning, I believe, helps you learn to be present, to feel better, and ultimately, to live your very best life.

Call to Action

How much time would you be willing to set aside each day in order to meditate? Morning? Afternoon? Both? What are your fears around meditation? Would you prefer a guided meditation or silence? What do you feel you would gain by being able to meditate? What are you waiting for?

10

GET ENOUGH SLEEP

Adolescents and young adults always roll their eyes at this one. I get it. I frequented bars at 2:00 a.m. and ate steak and cheese subs at three in the morning when I was in college. We know, though, that research shows our bodies need sleep; it skews the picture of true anxiety and depression if we don't get the proper amount. I don't know about you, but if I don't get enough sleep, I am not that nice. What are your healthy sleep hours?

Research shows we need seven to nine hours, which is true for me most nights. Some people can function on six. I recently read an article in *The Wall Street Journal* about a sleep class offered for students at Harvard. Some students reported they could go for days on very little sleep, not realizing sleep was so important. They reported that they caught up when they could. Please, don't do that. We are all driving beside you and others are working in your manic energy space. Sleep! Eight hours? Six? Find your zone. Make it happen.

Now, I understand, as both a therapist and a parent, some nights and phases are going to be less than ideal. Overall, though, make a conscious effort to get what you need and encourage your children to do the same. You emit a frequency that everyone around you needs to deal with during waking hours; it's not fair if you're not taking care of yourself by not getting enough sleep.

Call to Action

How much sleep do you require? How do you feel when you get less? How do you feel when you have a good night's sleep? What are you willing to do to get it? Choose to establish good sleep hygiene rituals each night (see #23, Practice Good Sleep Hygiene).

11

PLAY THE "AND THEN WHAT" GAME

Take it as far as you can go. For example, your anxious child says she can't go to school because what if she gets sick and throws up? Your response: "Ok, what if you did? Then what would happen?" Her: "I might throw up." You say: "Okay, then what would happen?" Her: "The janitor would clean it up." You: "And then what?" Her: "The nurse would call you." You: "And then what?" Her: "Then I'd go home and you'd take care of me." You: "Bingo." You can do this with your "inner child" as well.

Take the game as far as you can, all the way down the runway to where everything truly works out okay once you explore the potential outcomes and deal with possible scenarios in the rehearsal run. Most of the time, anxiety about the thing is worse than the thing. Teach your kids, and yourself, to run the anxiety all the way through to a place where you emerge unscathed, or at least laughing at yourself, because everything in the moment really is okay. Know you're safe by focusing on the present moment and not allowing your mind to run away with you, the way your gremlins would want you to.

Call to Action

What are the "what ifs" you tend to focus on? Play the "And Then What" game in your own mind. Can you take it as far as you can go? See how you feel with each "and then what?" Face the fear head on and then keep moving forward.

12

GET SOME EXERCISE

If you want to feel better—and release depression or anxiety symptoms in the best, most natural way possible—exercise.

It's that simple. Please don't say you don't have the time. If you mean business, you can free up twenty to thirty minutes in a day to increase your serotonin levels naturally, without side effects. Even though I consider myself a holistic therapist and encourage clients to do everything else first before taking medication, I am not against medication. I took antidepressants for two years in college. I can tell you this, though: exercise works just as well. Not once in a while, but a disciplined program.

If you say you don't have time, or make excuses, then I do not believe that you truly want to be well. If you genuinely want to stop suffering, you will do the 5-4-3-2-1 teachings of Mel Robbins (Melrobbins.com) and get up and get going. Like your life depends on it. It does. Commit to a mostly daily program. Thirty minutes is all you need. Your regimen doesn't have to be anything crazy. Yoga. Running. Walking. Six days a week is ideal as a remedy for depression, with one day of rest. Find a walking buddy or Meetup group to motivate you to stick to your plan. Exercise is not only natural Prozac; exercise grounds you, and helps you release negative buildup (that's why I do it every morning) and makes you feel better when you finish. Everyone I know feels better when they exercise. Just do it already. Get up and go. First thing is best. Then there're no excuses and it's ova!

Call to Action

What form of exercise do you prefer? What time of day feels best for you? What are you willing to do each day to raise your serotonin level naturally so that you feel less anxious and depressed? Exercise makes you feel good, soaring above anxious and depressed feelings. Get moving. Make no excuses.

13

DISCIPLINE YOURSELF

"Discipline" might be one of the most important words to add to your vocabulary if you want your blueprint to change. Tony Robbins, T.D. Jakes, Lisa Nichols, Eric Thomas, Jocko Willink, Rachel Hollis, Jaret Grossman and every other winner who speaks on the subject of motivation references the word discipline. You won't get anywhere unless you decide to take action and then back it up by doing what you said you would.

When you discipline yourself to work out, eat less sugar, change something that's not working, or learn something new, you're deciding to do the necessary work to get you to where you want to be. Discipline brings you to your preferred destination one intentional step at a time.

Schedule your time so you're productive and achieve results. There is tremendous power in productivity. Productivity gives you a leg up on the weight of anxiety and depression. But you have to show up. Little steps get things done. Being disciplined is the primary difference between those who do and those who wish to do.

Call to Action

Where could you be better disciplined? What big goal would you like to accomplish? What smaller goal? What steps could you take today to work toward each of those goals? Take each step and then reflect on how you feel as a result. What are you waiting for? Plan your start date.

BREATHE

Breathe deeply throughout the day, not just during meditation. Please invest in your own health first before you take care of everyone else. Yes, this includes your children. If you have young kids, I do not suggest you neglect your family responsibilities. What I mean looks like this: simply lie in bed in the morning and take a few minutes to breathe before you get up and start manically making your kids' lunches or cleaning the kitchen. Breathe before your kids get home from school, or when you get home from work, so you can separate one part of the day from the other, ready and refueled to deal with anything that comes your way. Breathe before appointments so your energy feels calm and less intrusive on other people. Breathe before you make a decision, taking the precious pause you need to be clear and sure of your intentions.

If you feel anxious the moment you open your eyes—a common complaint from my clients—or during the day when you are going, going, going, hold your hand over your heart. Breathe energy into your chest, blowing away that upper layer of tension like the weeds of a dandelion, and allow your heart room to rest. Give your heart the same love and attention you would to your children, your pets, or your partner when they're not feeling well. Apologize to your body for pushing it too hard. Tell your heart that you are learning to slow down in order to achieve balance and greater stability. This takes but a moment. So often we are barely breathing. Recognize this in yourself. Breathe.

Call to Action

Do you notice when your breathing becomes too fast and out of sync for your body's harmony? When do you notice you breathe too fast and feel rushed? Commit to taking a few deep breaths when you wake. Continue this practice throughout the day in order to tune in to how you feel, creating optimal health. How do you feel when you take deep breaths? Is this a practice you'd like to continue? Breathing brings calm. Choose to breathe consciously, with intention, to invoke calm in your life.

15

BEGIN AND END THE DAY
WITH GRATITUDE

Consider these your treasured bookends. When you first wake up, list three to five things you are grateful for in your journal or in your mind. Immediately. Do this before anything else. Most people wake up instantly feeling anxious, buzzing internally as if they're wired. By stating what you feel grateful for, you rise above the gremlin chatter in your mind. You cannot hold both a negative and a positive thought in your mind at the same time. Make your thoughts positive as soon as you realize they're negative.

Do not pick up your phone until you have identified five things you feel grateful for. Then, at the end of the day, list five things you feel grateful for a second time. Research shows that kids who focus on what they're grateful for at the end of each day have less anxiety and depression in their waking state. That means gratitude is good for adults, too. The practice of gratitude trains your mind to find what's good instead of what's negative. No gratitude is too small. Being grateful on a daily basis will cause you to witness measureable progress in this area after a few months.

Can't think of anything to be grateful for? How about the fresh sheets and warmth of your bed, food to eat, time with your children, your home, friends, your partner, heat, the birds outside your window waking you up to the day. Are we good? Even in your darkest moments, you can always, yes, always, find something going well. When you focus on what's going right, you feel better, which then kick-starts the process of abundance.

Call to Action

List three to five things you feel grateful for today. Then, again tonight after the day ends. Note how you feel. Gratitude begets gratitude. Start this practice today.

16

SET THE TONE FOR THE DAY FIRST THING IN THE MORNING

Lay the foundation for each day and you lay the foundation for your life. For you, this might mean sitting in prayer for a few minutes each morning, organizing your thoughts, stating five things you're grateful for, or simply focusing on how you want the day to go. Maybe you choose to exercise first to get your blood flowing and raise your serotonin level naturally. Whatever feels right to you, select an activity in those quiet moments before the day begins to connect with your thoughts—your highest thoughts—in order to start on elevated ground. If you check your phone before you check in with yourself, think about the negative message you're sending your mind and body. I've never had a client say, "That early morning routine you recommended? Yeah, that doesn't work." No one wants to get out of a warm bed. Yet, when you choose to start the day off right, you feel better for the entire day. Even, magically, when you haven't had the best night's sleep. How you start the day fuels the energy of your life, one twenty-four-hour period at a time.

PERSONAL SHARE

I begin each morning by sitting in meditation for five to twenty minutes, depending on the day, followed by thirty minutes of exercise. Yes, I am as busy as you are. I get up early to make this happen. Why? My morning routine helps me get in the best mind space like nothing else. I need that quiet time before life gets noisy. If you feel down or anxious in any way, then I highly encourage you to set the tone for your day first thing. I know it works, because I've done it long enough to know that I am a far better person when I do my morning routine than when I don't. Taking charge of your morning tells your negative thoughts that they're no longer steering the wheel.

Call to Action

What time would you have to awaken in order to take time for yourself, in order to clear your mind and start the day with intention—even for just five minutes? What would a perfect morning look like to you? What activity feels best? What activity would you like to start? What are you willing to commit to in order to start feeling better about your life? Make the choice to overcome anxiety and depression by getting up early.

17

STAY POSITIVE WITH AFFIRMATIONS

Affirmations help you rewrite your old, no-longer-serving narrative. Stating declarative sentences helps create a positive mindset, aligning you with what you want to have versus what you don't. When you affirm what you want, you reprogram your internal navigation system to overcome automatic negative thoughts. This technique takes time, but reaps massive benefits. When my clients consistently repeat and declare positive affirmations on a daily basis, they begin feeling better after a few months. You are reshaping your thoughts and your brain during this disciplined practice, and are far more able to easily dismiss the incessant chatter of your gremlin-speak and move on to better-feeling thoughts.

Affirmations look and sound like this: *I am living the life I want to live. I am in perfect health. I am surrounded by like-minded souls.* You can say positive statements proactively in the shower, during exercise (they're fueling during a run), on car rides, or while smack in the midst of negativity to immediately oppose a maladaptive thought. For example, when I am feeling frazzled, I immediately say, "I am calm." This works, though it takes practice, similar to lifting a five-pound dumbbell to work your biceps. You wouldn't say, "Oh, this isn't working" the first time you try. You need to give yourself time in order to see results. Stating affirmations is not about being unrealistic. It's a technique to raise the bar for your life, helping you move from one space into another. Try the practice yourself. By stating affirmations, you change your vibration to one you'd want to be a part of. Laying the groundwork for better thinking and feeling leads, more often than not, to the outcome you desire. I repeat, this works. Keep consistent in your practice to achieve results. Affirmations assist in manifesting what you want to come true.

Call to Action

Make a list of ten to twenty-five affirmations you'd like to think and feel on a daily basis. Start saying a number of them out loud, twice a day at least. I like the car ride to and from work to work on my affirmations. (No one knows you're talking to yourself. They'll just think you're on the phone.) Keep your list close so you can refer to it as a reminder of what you'd like to feel. Every day. This practice helps manifest what you want to have, by acting as if it's already happening, even when you can't see it yet. What are you waiting for? Start stating affirmations today.

18

PRACTICE MINDFULNESS

I use this exercise with clients who feel unsafe and struggle with the sense that they have lost control. Notice a particular color in the space around you. Count the circles, the squares, the red leaves falling to the ground in autumn. Pick one thing to focus on. Listen to the sound of the wind or feel the warmth of the sun on your face.

When you feel anxious, you feel like a balloon about to float away into the ether. To counter those feelings, concentrate on one thing. Find similar items in your space, like pens, cups, flowers, or furniture. Take the time to focus. Get out of your buzzing head and into your feet. When you feel a loss of control, it may look like your feet are on the ground, but most of your energy resides up in your head, which makes you feel panicked and unsafe. When you choose to be mindful, you redistribute that energy.

Call to Action

What mindfulness tool might you already be using? What new tools are you willing to try? Counting the circles? Staring out the window? The next time you feel nervous or anxious, try one of these exercises and note how you feel. Continue the practice. Be consistent. Mindfulness helps you to hold on, anchoring you to the present moment until you find your way.

19

KNOW YOUR "WHY"

In *Finding Your Own North Star,* Martha Beck writes, "The difference between success and failure isn't the absence of fear but the determination to pursue your heart's desires no matter how scared you are." Why do you want what you want? What does your main goal look like? Your dream place, relationship, or situation? Why? When you know why you want what you want, it becomes easier to stay focused and to eschew the non-important things in favor of the steps that will lead to your goal. When you know your why, the choice becomes far easier to talk back to your depression and anxiety, to see that darkness for what it truly is—an energy meant to keep you down and hold you back from your greatness. When you are clear about your why, the Universe, law of attraction style, now knows specifically what you want and immediately begins to work in your favor. Pay attention. When you know your why, opportunities are put in your path so you can more easily and effortlessly achieve what you desire. Decide your why and move in that direction each and every day.

Call to Action

Take a few minutes to consider why you want what you want. Is what you want for you or for someone else? To prove something to someone else? Simply feeding your ego? Try to get past the superficial reasons and search for the real reason you want what you do. When you know your true why, you can proceed with greater personal power. That's when you become aligned with an unstoppable force that begins to work for you. When you know your why, decide if you're willing to settle for anything less.

STAY CONNECTED

When you feel down or anxious, call, text, or email a friend to see yourself clearly, to get out of your own head, and to enter a healthier space. Not a friend who will agree with everything you say necessarily, but one who will challenge you and help you consider something you might not have considered before.

Different friendships and relationships serve various purposes. Know your go-tos when you need authentic connection, those people who make you feel better when you're in their presence. Connecting with others helps you to get out of your own story and the current chapter you're on, in order to listen to someone else's story, someone who just might help you rewrite your own by association.

Call to Action

Who are your go-tos when you need to connect? Who makes you feel better by being around them? Who makes you feel worse? Why? When can you schedule time with your person? Can you make this part of your regular schedule—weekly, monthly, or daily? Trust your intuition and find the rhythm that works best for you. Stick to it. Connect.

PART II

TAKE GOOD CARE OF YOURSELF

21

BE GOOD TO YOURSELF
EVERY DAY

A once-a-year getaway is a great idea, but that's a bonus. I'm talking every single day. Being good to yourself might simply be reading a good book every afternoon with a cup of green tea and dark chocolate (that's mine), going shopping and buying something new, exercising and eating well every day (more on that later), a nightly bath ritual, or watching your favorite comedic TV show in order to laugh and let go of the day's events.

What feels good to you each day might be something different. When dealing with anxious or depressed feelings, find one thing you can do to quiet the noise in your brain and treat yourself well. In college, a friend told me we need something to look forward to every day. Words to live by. Others? "Today is going to be a really, really good day," writes Louise Hay. Being good to yourself includes thinking good thoughts. For where thought goes, energy follows.

Call to Action

What does being good to yourself look like for you? How might you incorporate time for yourself every day? What are your three favorite ways to spend your time? Would you be willing to schedule one of them every day and schedule the other two throughout the week, at least once? How do you feel after you take this time for yourself? Make the choice each day to be good to yourself. Don't wait for someone else to do it for you.

22

GET OUT IN NATURE

Go outside. Daily. No matter the weather. Exercise outdoors when you can. Do yoga in your yard. Run. Walk. Even during the winter. Simply stepping outside and taking three deep breaths on your back steps when you let your dog out in the morning will do wonders for your mood. Nature heals. Fresh air immediately cleanses the energy buildup in your field from everything around you—overstimulation, excess activity, and toxic energy from people, places, and things.

Schedule time outside. If you are unable to do this on a regular basis, be conscious when you walk to your car or to your mailbox. Take sips of fresh air through an open window. It's amazing what nature can do for your body, mind, and spirit. Getting out in the great wide open, opening to the power of nature, and being truly present when you're there makes you realize the insignificance of little dramas, and how the Universe operates in perfect alignment without your help. Let the energy of nature raise your vibration.

PERSONAL SHARE

Every afternoon or evening when I leave my office, I stand by my car for a moment. I let the fresh air remove the buildup of anything accumulated from the day so that I can be clear for my family when I arrive home. I have done this ritual since I became a therapist.

Call to Action

When are you able to go outside during the weekdays? How about on the weekends? Where would you go? What could you let go of when you align with nature? Ask and ye shall receive. Make the choice to include the great outdoors in your schedule.

23

PRACTICE GOOD SLEEP HYGIENE

Sleep hygiene means preparing for sleep in a positive manner. For example, turn off your phone and any blue light at least thirty minutes before bed in order to wind down (TV, too), brush your teeth, shower, take a bath, get into comfy sleepwear, drink chamomile tea, warm milk with honey, or read to relax. Open the window a crack and sleep with the room as dark as possible. Use lavender on your pillow and in a diffuser by your bed for inspiration before you fall asleep. Clear yourself out for the night in order to let go of the day and prepare for sleep (see #30, Vacuum Meditation). Lastly, always list in your mind or in your journal what you're grateful for.

Call to Action

How do you prepare for sleep? How do you like to wind down? What three things would you be willing to add to your sleep routine in order to enjoy the process? Note how you feel the following morning. Decide what stays and what might need to be tweaked. Make your routine your own. Trust your gut.

24

TAKE SPACE

When you feel overwhelmed, take a moment to distance yourself from the area of injury, so to speak. I have my adolescent clients use this tool in school as part of creating a healthy toolbox, particularly when they feel a panic attack fast approaching. Spouses in a heated situation, leave the room before you say something you'll regret. And if you're someone who feels everyone else's stuff and avoids crowds for that very reason, otherwise known as a psychic empath, *take space*—go somewhere where there isn't a lot of stimulation, like the bathroom, or back in your car, to gather your thoughts.

Know how you feel. When everything feels like too much, it's too much. There's no need for explanation. You are honoring your body and what *you* need to feel better. In *Counseling with Choice Theory*, William Glasser wrote, "When people choose painful or crazy symptoms, it's not because they enjoy them. It's because they don't know anything better to do." Choose different behavior by taking space the next time you feel socially awkward or overwhelmed. Simply step away from the situation, regroup, and then decide on your next best move. Choose to move through the wall that keeps you back from more powerful mental health.

Call to Action

What places and situations bring up the need to take space? What is your game plan the next time you find yourself in a situation that feels like too much? What is the dominant emotion you feel when you require space? What does that tell you about yourself and what you might need? Make your needs a priority. What are you waiting for?

25

DECLUTTER YOUR SPACE

Have you heard of Marie Kondo, author of *The Life-Changing Magic of Tidying Up*? My goodness, that woman is a dynamo in terms of powerful mental health. Kondo has taken her OCD and made it work for her in the best way possible. Take Kondo's advice and declutter your closet, your home, your whole life with the intention of clearing to open to something better. I have clients do this before big events in order to release old energy that might be blocking their progress. When you clear a space, you immediately feel the effects when you walk into that new, lighter energy. Make this exercise fun.

Grab a trash bag and have someone help you if you need support. Bless each item for when and how it might have supported you in the past and then let that old, stale energy go.

Call to Action

What needs to go in your space now that you've decided you want to feel better? What might you like to add? Set aside ten minutes a day for this activity. Set the timer, and toss what no longer represents who you are or what you want. If the item brings up anxious feelings or has a low vibration, GET RID OF IT. Let it go. Feel the lightness that comes as a result. Open to new feelings. Journal how you feel—from guilt, to angst, to light as a feather. Open to new ways of being.

26

DO WHAT YOU LOVE

Here's what's true: If you are not doing what you love to do each day, you will feel depressed. Shocking, isn't it? If you're doing work that doesn't feel filled with purpose, you will feel out of alignment with your highest self. In turn, you will feel grumpy and irritable, upset with your kids, your spouse, yourself. Your body will experience stomachaches, inflammation, and other psychosomatic symptoms. Conversely, when you do what you love, you will feel happy, physically well, energized, and passionate about life.

Do what you love. Start today. Think about what you love doing and move in that direction. If you are an adult who would prefer a different job than the one you have, take time every day—even fifteen minutes—to read up on other opportunities, strategizing ways to get you to where you want to be. If you are a child still in school who detests getting up every morning, come home and research the topic you'd rather be studying, or how about learning a new hobby or trade? Spend conscious time daydreaming about what you'd rather be doing.

What you want, the Universe wants too. As Paolo Coelho writes, "When you want something, all the Universe conspires to help you achieve it." Believe. Decide what you love and spend time each day aligning with that area of focus, even if you can't imagine how it will all work out.

Call to Action

What do you do each day that might make you feel anxious or depressed? What might you be able to eliminate? What do you do each day that makes you feel happy? How can you make changes to get closer to what you want? Think of one step you can take today to move in that direction. What the heck are you waiting for?

27

PRACTICE SELF-CARE

Take good care of yourself. Do the simple things. Exercise, get your hair cut on a regular basis, eat foods that do you right, spend time with others to stay connected to the people you love. Simply do the things you need to do to be well. Anxiety and depression have a much harder time creeping into your space when you practice self-care.

To me, self-care means balancing activities, like working, and then resting. Thursdays are my late nights seeing clients, so on Fridays I write, read, and rest. On Fridays, I barely talk at all. I also focus on balanced eating. Whenever I binge eat—where my addictive tendencies spend most of their time these days—I'll have smoothies for meals one or two days during the week.

Know yourself and what *you* need. Personally, I try to limit the time I spend with people who drain me. I schedule chiropractic and acupuncture appointments on a fairly regular basis, sleep and eat to the best of my abilities, spend time with friends who lift me, connect with people who inspire me, even if that's by listening to a podcast or a motivational video while I'm on my runs. That to me is self-care, beyond the basics of brushing your teeth, showering, and getting dressed each day. Self-care means paying attention to what you need, when, and how often. Are you feeling particularly extroverted? Schedule time with friends. Are you feeling the need to retreat? Then get good at saying no. Your body, mind, and spirit will thank you later.

Call to Action

What does self-care look like for you? What do you do to be well? What does physical self- care look like for you? Mental? Spiritual? Emotional? If you were practicing good self-care on every level, what would you do daily? Weekly? Monthly? Yearly? What can you start doing today for self-care? Schedule your ideas. No excuses.

28

SCHEDULE REGULAR MENTAL HEALTH DAYS

We all need time off from the daily grind. One of my personal visions is for people to plan scheduled retreat time on a regular basis to avoid ending up in a hospital when they're depleted, exhausted, and waaaay past their endurance—hospitals being the exact opposite environment of what your soul needs when true mental and emotional rest is required.

Take days off when you need them. Schedule monthly mental health days—a day to look forward to, in order to rest and refuel. True mental health days might include limiting (or zero) social media. Focus on reading, watching good movies, journaling about how things are going and where you want to find yourself at the end of the month or the end of the year. Take a walk. Take a spiritual inventory. Nap. Regroup. Eat well or eat comfort food, whatever feels right, but take the time you need. Don't just wait until you're having a bad day. Schedule a day ahead of time. I shoot for a day each month to shut out the world and rest.

PERSONAL SHARE

My first good quality mental health day started during grad school. I began my master's training while raising two small children and wondered, during that first class, what in the name of God I had gotten myself into. Complete cognitive dissonance.

After that first semester ended, I told my husband I needed to take off the day after Christmas. I planned the day in bed, to read something other than textbooks and to rest (also to eat the rest of the chocolate raspberry cake that I made for Christmas from O Magazine). Having that day helped my drained mind and body so much—after not having had formal education for over ten years—that after spending most of the day in bed and eating that leftover cake, I got up, reenergized and refueled, and proceeded to build one of those hard-to-put-together toy sets with a million pieces that my son got for Christmas. All by myself.

If you know me well, building things, putting things together, doing things with my hands, or reading manuals of any kind is not a skill I possess. But that day, after a full day of rest, I headed to the basement and put the entire thing together on my own, much to the shock of my husband. I felt proud of that moment and even prouder of the fact that I had asked for a mental health day. Ask yourself, what might be the consequences if you don't?

Call to Action

When was the last time you took a day off? What did you do with your time? What might you do differently next time? What would be the perfect mental health day for you? When can you schedule a day? Are you able to schedule monthly time, even if just for a morning or afternoon? Weekends work too. Schedule time. Days off do wonders for remedying negative feelings.

29

MORNING JOURNALING

Julia Cameron's *The Artist's Way* reminds us to "show up to the page," one of my favorite sayings, which also happens to be a metaphor for life. Empty yourself by journaling in the morning. By not carrying around anything from yesterday, and years past, you can release your thoughts and start the day with an empty cup.

I love the three-page instructions Cameron suggests, though at this point in my life, I don't always make the time for three pages. I do write a page or so in my journal most mornings, a practice I have honored for twenty years. My journaling starts with scribbling down the rapid content of my dreams; unraveling their messages; working out my thoughts, ideas, and goals for the day; and listing five things I'm grateful for. By journaling each morning, you dramatically decrease the odds of wrestling with anxiety by dealing with your stuff head on. Besides, journaling the content of your dreams reveals fascinating information (see #63, Consult Your Dreams). Once you open that portal, dreams bring to light subconscious knowledge, knowledge that can help you transform your negative emotions. By choosing to journal, listening to what your dreams have to say, you're saying yes, versus no, to your life.

Call to Action

What time would you have to get up in the morning to journal before starting your day? What would you like to release? How do you think you would feel if you emptied yourself mentally every morning? Write down any dreams you remember and any interpretation or intuition about the messages they carry. Write down what you are grateful for and what you intend to do for the day, setting your intention. You'll be amazed at how you'll be reminded throughout the day by your subconscious mind to accomplish the things you said you would.

30

VACUUM MEDITATION

This exercise takes you through your body at the end of the day and clears out what you don't need. Think of this as an advanced tighten and release (see #5). Start by lying on your back in bed. Imagine a hand-held vacuum coming in through the top of your head, operated by an angel or ancestor of your choice, whose nightly job is to help you move toward perfect health.

Picture the hand-held vacuum cleaning out your mind, your face, your neck and shoulders and the stress you often hold in that area, down your chest, your torso, your legs, and out the soles of your feet. Slowly, methodically, move through your body, vacuuming away stress, illness, toxic energy, dis-ease. When you are done, imagine a cocoon of golden healing light surrounding your now-clear body, healing you while you sleep.

Call to Action

Make the last thing before you go to bed be the Vacuum Meditation. Picture the vacuum taking away your worries and stress, allowing you to relax and sleep in the clearest state possible. How do you feel during the exercise? How do you feel about the idea that this is possible? Remind yourself to do this nightly. Notice how you feel. Notice how you wake up and whether your mind tends to feel clearer as a result. Making the choice to clear your mind on a nightly basis creates stronger mental health.

31

SCHEDULE TIME TO FOCUS ON YOUR KEY AREAS

Typically we have four to six key areas where we spend our time and energy: family, health, work, friends/social, spiritual, and YOU time. Once a week, schedule your time deliberately in these key areas, sitting down perhaps on Sundays to map out the week ahead. Address each area of your life and make sure to spend your time wisely. The idea of weekly planning serves to map out your life in the way *you* want your world to look and feel—not dictated to you by someone else's schedule. Decide for each key area where and how you will devote time each day to spending energy toward things that matter.

Want to write a book? You might have to plug in an hour a day early in the morning, or late at night, or wherever you can throughout the week. For work, write down the hours you spend on the job each day and then decide what you want to do with the time left. Then move to the next key area. When do you connect with family? Not just standing in the same space—when do you plan time to be emotionally available to talk and check in with your children or your significant other? Plan time to watch TV with your spouse, to talk with your kids, or more importantly, to listen.

Schedule this time so that at the end of each day and the end of the week, you have spent your time in ways that are productive and important. No, this doesn't have to be perfect, and you can certainly forward things in each day that you have yet to do. We're not going for perfection; we're simply making sure we give energy to those things that matter most.

For example: if you need to ride your mountain bike to feel happy, make sure you schedule in the time, three to four times a week if that's your rhythm. Know where you are absolutely going to carve out that time so you can have MORE energy for the other things you need to do. Have to ride at 5:00 a.m. in your orange neon gear? I promise you, you will have more energy the rest of the day. I wrote the outline for my first book from 4 a.m. to 6 a.m. every weekday morning for months, and I swear I had more energy during that time than I did before I started writing. When you make time for activities that are most important to you, you create a formula for success. It's harder to feel down when you are experiencing success!

Call to Action

Sit down on Sundays in a clear space. Get a cup of tea or coffee and your favorite pen. List the four to six most important areas of your life. How will you make time for each one daily and weekly, starting this week? How do you think you'll feel at the end of the week when you look back? Take the ten minutes or so it takes to create your schedule each Sunday and enjoy creating the life you want. This action step should be fun and one of your favorite activities—it's designing your life the way you want to! Who else would you want to design your life?

32

LISTEN TO YOUR ANXIETY

Anxiety doesn't always feel comfortable, but ultimately makes you move toward what you're supposed to be doing to live your best life. In *The Land of Blue,* I use a metaphor for anxiety called the "energy of the bees." That energy that feels itchy and uncomfortable—yet assists you in getting to where you say you want to go.

When you learn to read the energy of anxiety and what it's telling you—that very first impression of what you feel, what you know you need to do—you can move way from old self-destructive behaviors (the bottle, overspending, picking at your skin, biting your nails, or popping pills). I have come to believe that anxiety is good at its core: coaxing you to choose alternative behaviors by providing contrast to how you feel when you keep delaying your desires. Anxiety offers you a glimpse of an alternate reality, if only you'd listen to what anxiety has to say, to the real whisper underneath the discomfort. Be brave the next time you feel anxious. Be still and learn to read the energy in the discomfort. Anxiety very often serves your life.

Call to Action

When was the last time you felt really anxious and your anxiety helped you move away from a bad situation or get out of danger? Do you recognize how anxiety, by its very nature, strengthens your intuition? When do you feel anxious? What do you feel the anxiety might be telling you? Close your eyes and ally with the energy. See if you can picture a face, a gender, a guide, a color, a scene before your eyes that brings forth a message of what you might need to do. Yes, you can do this exercise. Anyone can. Deciphering the message of anxiety simply takes practice and wanting to.

33

KNOW YOUR TRIGGERS

If Sunday night causes you to panic about the upcoming workweek, come up with a new regimen. Watch your favorite show, eat your favorite foods, surround yourself with those you love, create a schedule you look forward to early Monday morning: running or meditating while listening to Deepak Chopra or Oprah Winfrey.

In *Warning: Psychiatry Can Be Hazardous to Your Mental Health*, William Glasser wrote, "Choosing leads to solving problems." *Do something different* to make your situation, and thus, your thoughts about the situation, different. Should certain people give you a stomachache when you're around them, guess what? Right. Step back, spend less time, cut them out altogether if the shoe fits. C.C. Chapman, in his authentic and practical advice-giving book, *Amazing Things Will Happen,* calls these people ankle biters. His advice? "Never reply to ankle biters, no matter what they say." Don't waste your time. Trust that something is happening here, that you are being instructed to go in a different direction. *Know your triggers.* If you keep dealing with your triggers in the same old way, you become part of the problem. Yes, I'm talking to you. The triggers happen for a reason, to help you behave differently, like you said you wanted to. Trust the process and how things show up in your life after you set your intention for change.

Call to Action

What are your biggest triggers? How do you deal with them now? What could you do differently the next time you feel triggered? Advanced-level question: How could you ally with your triggers in order to dance with them differently? Be brave and move forward.

34

REFRAME YOUR SITUATION

If you tend to engage in self-destructive behaviors, like biting your nails when you're doing something that's difficult, or your thoughts simultaneously barraging you with *I don't know how to do this; therefore, I'm stupid,* attempt to reframe your situation.

For example, if you are a student and you struggle with math and wrestle with homework every night until you, and everyone else around you, is miserable, step back and consider a new way of thinking. Cause here's the thing: if your calling was to be a mathematician, you would be LOVING math, or at least stimulated by the challenge of solving an equation. If you're not experiencing those positively charged, mentally stimulating emotions, guess what? You're not here to teach the rest of us how to do math! That's good news! You just figured out what you are not here on this Earth to do, which is just as important, in my opinion, as figuring out what you are here to do. I'm not suggesting you blow off math homework, because you do have to get through your various subjects, it's part of the process of going to school, but you can reframe your thoughts in the midst of your misery by saying something like, "Wow, I have no clue how to do this and I really detest geometry. Good thing I've figured out I'm not here to be a mathematician. I'll just get through this, do my best, ask for help if I need to, and then move on to what I really enjoy doing." Reframe your situation to create a different feeling.

For example, whenever I have to do something with technology, and I can't figure it out because my brain doesn't work that way and I'm hitting the printer button over and over in frustration, stating in my mind F*** THIS, and then my husband yells from the other room, "You're gonna print that out for six months!" I eventually take a deep breath and tell myself, "Girl, these are not your skills, they never will be, and you couldn't care less. This is one of the many reasons why you have the husband you have, and why there are people in the world who long to be hired because of these complementary skills, thus, contributing to the harmony of us all."

Reframe your difficult situation so you can get out of the frustrated feelings that lead to more intense anxiety and depressed symptoms. Choose to move through the wall that blocks you from making progress. You're the only one who can.

Call to Action

What do you feel negatively about? How could you reframe the situation and your consequential thoughts? How do you feel when you reframe your situation out loud? How do you feel when you see it in writing? Are you able to see what you're good at and what you bring to the table? List five to ten of your skills. Say them out loud and feel the way it feels. Now move forward.

35

FIND THE GOOD

It's always there.

If you don't like the space you're standing in, think of what might be going well. What might be happening that's positive at the moment? Do you have a best friend? Do you have a pet you adore? Are you healthy? Are you in a job you love?

Instead of focusing on all that might be going wrong with your life, call to mind something good. I recall a client who detested his job. He spent an enormous amount of time focused on all that he couldn't stand about his current line of employment. When I asked him what might be going well, he answered, "I have a beautiful wife and family. A gorgeous home. I like six or seven people I work with. My schedule allows me to be at all of my kids' sporting events, and I get to play golf about three times a week." Everything else was great, he said, except the job. Hmmmm. Now I'm not minimizing the discomfort of being at a job you don't like, but if we spend most of our time hyper-focused on what we don't like, guess what? Right. We'll get more of it, missing out on everything else that might be going great.

Call to Action

List three things you are unhappy about in the moment. Now list five things that are good. Right now. No matter where you are or what you are doing. Notice how you feel when you think about the good things. Give yourself five minutes to think about what you might be able to do about the not-so-good things and then spend the rest of the time focusing on what's going right. Note the difference. Decide for yourself, in the way you feel, which you'd rather spend your time thinking about.

36

TALK BACK TO YOUR GREMLINS

Yup, they're back. If the negative voice in your head drones on and on about what a loser you are (don't worry, the gremlins say that to all of us), decide for yourself if you're okay with that. That's right. You decide if you want to buy what your gremlins are selling. The choice is yours.

Do the work to free yourself from that gremlin prison and bust through that wall. Yes, you can. I swear to God, if I can do it, anyone can. If you don't do the work, though, you're susceptible to staying in victim mode, and victim mode for too long fuels the energy of anxiety and depression. Newsflash: That's what your gremlins want for you. Are you okay with that?

Call to Action

What do your gremlins say to you most often? If you have OCD, what does your OCD tell you to do? For example, "If you're not perfect, things won't be okay," which really is an out-and-out lie. How can you talk back to your OCD or gremlins? What are you willing to do the next time they trespass in your space? How will you feel when you choose not to listen, to move through the wall and emerge on the other side, even just one time? Stand in that feeling. What are you waiting for?

37

LAUGH

My late mother-in-law was a master at this. Laughter truly is the best medicine. You know those people—you just stop to think about them and the last time you got together, and you start laughing in the best way possible. Call them or text them right now and recall a funny memory, or plan a night so you have their company to look forward to. I realize this might be hard when you're struggling, but reaching out is exactly what you need to do during those times. Put a date on your calendar.

Norman Cousin's *Anatomy of an Illness*—a great little book—stresses this strategy. Cousins wrote about healing himself with laughter—how after being ill he chose to go home and watch funny movies versus lying in a hospital bed, and how this technique, along with a few other alternative methods, including a heavy dose of Vitamin C, cured his illness. Now, that's healing. Laughter really might be the best remedy for our ailments, both physical and emotional. I always feel better after I've spent time laughing with my cousins, my husband and kids, and my closest friends when we just hang out, eat food, and laugh about nonsense.

Call to Action

Who makes you laugh? How often do you laugh? Make this part of your life if you truly want to feel better. Ask yourself this: Will laughter make me feel good? Of course it will. Make the choice. Today.

SLOW DOWN

I once worked with a client who commented that he never ate in a rush—he'd rather wait than eat in a frenzied state. I remember shifting in my chair, silently instructing that shadow part of my personality, *that is so right, you need to do that.* Slow down. Pause. Think. Then decide what you want, what you truly want. When you don't, you react, which feeds anxiety like fish feed sharks because your mind then tends to ruminate over the reckless, impulsive things you said or did as a result of reacting. Slow. Your. Car. Down. You won't ever regret slowing down long enough to make a more conscious decision.

Have you ever noticed that people in positions of power—true power—have slower, and greater control over, their speech? Emulate that. Breathe and pause and then speak, from the heart this time, simultaneously stomping on your anxiety and depressed feelings that want you to keep doing like you do.

Call to Action

When do you rush? When do you eat and drink unhealthy foods? When you don't have time? All the time? Decide when and how you'll slow yourself down so you make better choices and move toward becoming the person you want to be in this lifetime. Start today. If it helps, talk out loud and tell someone, "Hold on, I'm trying something new here, and slowing myself down to see other paths I might want to take." They might find this behavior weird, or they might find this new behavior inspiring and apply this strategy to their own life. Choose to be an influencer by being real.

39

READ FOR INSPIRATION

Reading words of inspiration each day helps you feel better. Read biographies of people who have done what you want to do, who have done what you could never imagine doing, who got over the hardships of their lives and learned to turn things around.

Listen to podcasts of people doing what they love, who are victorious at the game of life. Learn their strategies, their triumphs, their failures, and then heed their advice. Read, listen, and lean in so you can more easily emulate those whose stories inspire you. Take what you need from each book and leave the rest behind. Read just a page a day from books kept beside your bed. Take a few minutes to feed your soul with words.

Call to Action

Whose life do you resonate with? Who interests you? If you could "be" anyone, who would that be? Why? Check out books that call to you, learning how the authors became who they are today. A great story typically lies in the wake of people who have achieved true success. Choose to read. Today.

40

DRESS FOR SUCCESS

Decide what your clothes say about you and how you want to represent yourself. I pick certain colors for each month. It's part of my creativity, choosing a theme and (mostly) sticking to colors that resonate with me for the month I'm in. As a writer, I tend to opt for the comfiest clothes when at home working beside my bulldog. When I'm in therapist mode, I dress more stylishly. No matter the role, how you present yourself is an important choice you make in transforming the way you feel.

When you look like you care enough about yourself to put yourself together, you are choosing to present a more confident version of yourself to the world. Shop when your clothes become too big or too small. Replace your shoes when they're worn. If you want people to see you as successful and to feel like a person who possesses strong mental health, take the time to dress that way. Act as if.

The night before you go to work or school, choose your outfit. Think about your day and how you want to show up. One of the cards in my *Planting the Seeds* deck for kids, states, "Choose the Colors of Your Outfit To Express Yourself." What colors do you feel like wearing?

What do you want your clothes to say about you? Be creative in your dress, hairstyle, or makeup. Watch how people are drawn to you as a result. If you're simply staying around the house, then own the sweats or pajamas you wear. Or put on a pair of favorite jeans, ones that make you feel like yourself. Get comfy and cozy in whatever you wear, but bring intention to your outfit. There's a difference.

As Marie Kondo writes in *The Magic of Tidying Up*, if you haven't worn something in a year, bless the item for who you once were when you wore that particular dress, pantsuit, or pair of pajamas, and then toss the piece in the trash bin. This is a liberating exercise for releasing who you were then and opening to who you want to become.

PERSONAL SHARE

In college, during my clueless days, I used to wear these tan-colored pants I was required to wear at the bar where I worked as a waitress. Apparently, they were too big on me. I had no clue about fashion and I wore mostly sweatpants, not being particularly fond of my body at that time. One night, at an employee holiday get-together, I wore a pair of jeans, to which one of my colleagues, and friends, replied, "Oh my God, I've never seen you in jeans; you look great." I felt as if a frying pan hit me over the head. Unbeknownst to me, my tan work pants were *huge* and I didn't realize that fact because I didn't care enough about myself to dress in a way that flattered me. Oh, silly girl. My point? Dress for success. You're worth it. Plus, you raise the vibration of your outer landscape when you do. What you bring to the world you get back. If you dumb down, or dress like you don't care, the outer world reflects those feelings back to you. Trust me.

Call to Action

What do you tend to wear to work? At home? Out to dinner with friends? What are your roles and how do you dress for each? What colors do you tend to wear? I tend to wear certain colors on certain days, and set my colors at the beginning of each month, not strictly but mostly. What fabrics, colors, and styles do you admire? What changes would you like to make in your life to reflect who you are and who you'd like to become? What's one step you can take in that direction? What would you toss? Why? What would you be saying good-bye to? What could you bring into your life as an exchange? Move forward with conviction.

PART III

BELIEVE

41

PAY ATTENTION TO THE SIGNS

When you feel anxious or depressed, signs are hard to hear, see, or feel. However, the spiritual signs are all around you, all the time, reminding you that you're watched over, being guided to your greatness, and that everything in this moment really is okay.

Signs like that bird at just the right time, that phone call from someone who's been thinking about you, or that literal sign on the side of the road that says STOP—just when you're thinking for the thousandth time that day that nothing good ever lasts. Signs are from Spirit. Yes, they are. Signs remind you to pay attention to when things flow—a green light from the Universe—and when they don't.

Have you ever recalled the little whisper you heard in your head the first time you met someone, and felt that magnetic pull of attraction, yet you knew there was something off, a little red flag, but you chose to ignore the warning sign and move forward with the relationship anyway? Yeah. How did that work out for you? Me, not so good either.

On the flip side, recall that feeling of *this is a definite yes, do that, go on that retreat, make that call, risk looking foolish*. That's how I started actively working with my intuition, calling detectives on cold cases almost twenty years ago, risking that feeling of looking like an absolute idiot. I trusted the signs I was receiving to make those phone calls; more often than not, I was surprised and validated by the detectives' receptivity.

Listen to the signs. Trust them. Signs are meant to guide you and your life. They require no explanation to anyone else. The best part? The signs are ALWAYS there.

Call to Action

When was the last time you received a sign? Was the sign positive or negative? How did things turn out? What would you have to do to pay attention to the signs in your life? What are you waiting for? Stay open to the signs. Watch how they work in your life and in your favor.

42

PRAY

What is your spiritual practice? Spirituality doesn't necessarily mean religion. Praying can be done in many different ways. The act of connecting to something greater than your self is what's important.

Praying represents an act of faith, trusting that our life serves as part of the larger puzzle.

When you pray, you believe a force guides your life, a force that knows far better than you do. When you pray, you give yourself over to the spiritual, asking God—or the Universe or Nature, whatever your belief—to help you, to take away your troubles, so you can focus on making the most of the twenty-four hours of your day, trusting you are heard.

Spirituality is a private and personal experience. Pray in the way you see fit—regardless of how your upbringing told you to pray—but not just when you need something. Make prayer a daily discipline. Walk in the woods, attend church or temple, meditate after yoga. However you practice, practice prayer. Parents, teach your children to pray. Give them a spiritual foundation, and your kids will be far more emotionally secure in their lives. Even if you think they're not listening when they're young, children often come back to spiritual teachings as adults, building on the foundation their parents provided.

Call to Action

What is your faith practice? What would you like it to be? When do you pray? How? Include prayer in your schedule this week. Today.

43

CHANGE THE STORY IF YOU "CAN'T" CHANGE YOUR SITUATION

Some people are in a job or relationship they can't get out of at the moment. Sometimes, that's simply the way life is. If you truly need to stay in a job you detest, or aren't ready or willing to get out of a relationship that brings you down, your other option is to change the story you tell yourself about the work you're doing or about the relationship that drains you.

Perhaps, instead of focusing on what's wrong about the job, you focus on rewriting a more positive narrative: the paycheck your job provides, the one person you connect with, the ride to and from that allows you to listen to motivational podcasts and audiobooks. Whatever the current story, create a new one. The action step to feel better can be that simple.

Understand the story you're telling yourself is a mindset. If you don't like how you feel about your current story, rewrite the narrative. For example, take a negative sentence like, "I'll never get anywhere in this position. This is a dead-end path," and rewrite the script to, "Today I start fresh, grateful for the mindless work I do here so I can dream about where I want to be." How you think about your situation creates the outer landscape you see. Create a better view by rewriting the story you want to tell.

Call to Action

What story are you telling yourself about your job? What are the pros? What are the cons? What new story are you willing to write? How would that make you feel? List three things you can focus on now about your job, or your situation, until you make the positive changes in your life that you need to make.

44

OPEN THE DOOR IN THE WALL

Let's go more in-depth with the visualization and imagination piece that have become an essential part of my own practice, in addition to my work with clients. This might be my favorite way to beat depressive thoughts and anxious feelings, if I had to pick one. Rumi writes, "Why do you stay in prison when the door is so wide open?"

When you feel stuck or anxious or like every crevice in your body is filled with fear, picture yourself standing behind that looming grey wall. Then, imagine a doorknob in the wall that you can open with ease. Walk through the door, stepping past the wall, letting yourself out from that previously stuck space. Yeah. Just like that. Yup. Just like that. My shoulders are relaxed just sitting here writing about that simple, powerful step, because it's worked so many times for my clients when they realize how simple letting yourself out of that personal prison can be. Remember, even when you don't know what to do once you get to the other side, anything's better than those awful feelings of being held hostage.

Choose to step beyond that threatening, dark energy. Let your mind catch up to the new behavior. Your gremlins will freak—their intention is strictly to hold you back from your greatness—and try to crawl all over you like white on rice, but that's okay, because you'll have already exited the building.

Call to Action

What self-imposed prison do you long to let yourself out of? Picture the prison, the wall, in specific detail. Now visualize a doorknob at hand level. Reach for it. Turn the knob and step out into the open. Feel your body respond. When your thoughts tell you that it's impossible, made up, or too magical for your adult brain to believe, talk back and tell them, "Too late, I'm already gone." Believe.

45

SPEND TIME WITH THOSE YOU LOVE AND WHO LOVE YOU

I don't mean those who talk down to you or who you drink and do drugs with because that's the only thing you have in common. Choose those people who really love you, the strong and the weak parts of you, for all that you are. Who lifts you? Who makes you laugh, the crack-up belly-laugh kind, and who respects your individual choices? Your true friends honor you, your quirkiness, your rituals, your habits, and your time. Choose wisely.

Honor that intuitive feeling you receive when you're in the presence of someone who really gets you. You know the feeling in the way you converse. There are no pretenses. You feel authentically yourself and free to be who you really are. In contrast, when you're with someone you don't feel that way with, you feel judged, nervous, or anxious (which might actually be their energy, more on that later). You might stutter, say socially awkward things, and tend to ruminate after you leave the space of someone who isn't aligned with you. That's not what we're going for.

When you spend time with people who make you feel judged, don't beat yourself up. Congratulate yourself for figuring out what you don't want so you can then choose what you do want. You can certainly give a pass to people for their moods, we're all human beings after all, but I like to say, three strikes and you're out. Usually, I tend to go with two now—that's become the new rules of my game.

Call to Action

Who in your life makes you feel better when you're around them? Can you plan to spend more time together? Even talking over the phone? Who can you say no to, understanding that by making that choice, you're consciously rising above negativity? List your top five to ten peeps and insert these people into your weekly schedule to reinforce your intention. Schedule your time to be around people who give you that none-other feeling of authentic connection.

46

SPEND TIME WITH FAMILY

Spend time with family members—the good ones. This section does not include friends on purpose, strictly family. I realize this one's tricky because family often triggers your anxious and depressed feelings. Isolating from them all, though, doesn't always work, and can cause you to feel really lonesome. Would you consider seeking the grey area? I come from a long line of grudge holders on one side. (I'll keep which side to myself.) I can shut people out like nobody's business. It's an inherent skill. (I might even be a master, but that'd be bragging.) Over time, though, especially after having children, I've learned not to.

If someone in your family is truly toxic, then that makes sense. But if certain family members simply annoy you or have certain behaviors that drive you nuts (I used to make my grandmother walk out to the rock wall on my property to have a cigarette), then consider accepting your family members for the good they give, the memories you share, and who they are at their core. Once you have children, it's important that they know their family. Generations are there to learn from, both what to do and what not to do. Part of feeling better comes from accepting both the good and poor attributes of those we love. And how about the cousin connection? Stories and memories, good and bad, make for hours of conversation and fun at family gatherings. Cousins know you and your family, with all the dysfunction, better than anyone else. Take comfort in that. Create a space for the grey area and move forward.

Call to Action

Who are the keepers in your family? How can you spend more time together? What event could you initiate? What might you agree to attend? Choose what feels right and do that knowing you are moving forward in a lighter space. Believe.

47

PET THERAPY IS THE BEST THERAPY

Animals soothe. Regardless of whether it's a dog, cat, or gerbil, when you have something you need to care for other than yourself, you get out of yourself and into the unconditional love only an animal can give. Pets love like no other: there's no back talk, they don't leave clothes on the floor, they don't complain about stupid stuff that means nothing in the big scheme of things, and although they may slobber on the floor after they drink, they don't care what you have or how you look today. They simply love. I adore my bulldog, and the ones we've had before him. I love the companionship, the loyalty, the comfort, and the care, which goes both ways. Animals love consistently and genuinely all the time.

Call to Action

Do you have a pet? If not, how might you bring one into your life? If you "can't" have a pet due to living arrangements or allergies, how might you connect with the love of an animal? Can you watch animal YouTube videos? Take a dog from the local shelter for a walk? If you do have a pet, how much love are you giving them on a daily basis? How much time do you spend playing, walking, petting, and snuggling up on the couch watching a movie? Pets offer a cure for blue feelings just by being themselves. Take the time.

48

FORGIVE

You probably knew you were going to see this one on the list. My best friend and rock-star relationship coach Laurie McAnaugh (www. lauriemcanaugh.com) brings forgiveness into her work by helping men and women become more powerful versions of themselves. *Forgiveness is key.*

Nelson Mandela once said, "Resentment is like drinking poison and then hoping it will kill your enemies." When you feel angry at someone, *you* hold that negative, toxic energy in YOUR body, which hurts YOU—not the other person. I believe that the message of Jesus—one of the greatest teachers to ever walk this Earth—of forgiveness and doing unto others as we'd have done to us is of utmost importance. You must forgive.

It is for you that you forgive. Forgiving releases toxic feelings from your body, versus holding in negative emotions that often lead to physically feeling unwell. Speak calmly to the person you feel angry at if this is a viable option, or write about your anger— write a letter you'll never send, tearing it up into a thousand pieces when you're done, but *let it go.*

Use your visualization skills and picture a mass of darkness leaving your chest area—typically where we hold anger and resentment— and allow it to dissipate, swirling up into the air the way smoke looks after blowing out a candle. Let any resentment leave, really leave, up into the ether, out of your energy field.

Another tip when you're in the act of forgiveness: send light to the other person. Like fairy dust, imagine in your mind tossing light around the person who hurts you or drives you nuts, inevitably pulling you away from being present and more powerful. You may have to do this five hundred times. In. A. Row. That's okay; send light anyway. You can say, "Take this from me, God. You'll deal with this better than I ever could."

If you need further inspiration, listen to the late, great Wayne Dyer's backstory. Dyer forgave his father, at his father's gravesite, after years of holding onto anger. As soon as he released and forgave, Dyer went on to write his first book, *Your Erroneous Zones,* a book that became a bestseller. I believe the souls of those who hurt you are actually waiting for you to forgive, that they're learning and evolving too—whether here on this plane or on the other side. In order to raise your consciousness, and maybe theirs too, you might choose to practice forgiveness. Trust what feels right and when to forgive.

PERSONAL SHARE

An example of how forgiving has shown up in my own life: I wrote about my maternal grandfather in *The Land of Blue.* My grandfather wasn't a bad person. He simply had his faults and quirks, the way all people do in the dynamic of dysfunctional families. Those quirks inspired the character Grandpa Jack in the novel. Then, something really cool happened at the end of my writing. My grandfather came to me in a dream and asked me to add something at the end of the book, something positive to convey the good in him, too, not just the dysfunction. When I woke from that moving, humbling dream, I honored my grandfather's request and immediately felt his pride.

Later, another cool thing happened. I received a reading from a skilled medium who told me, "Your grandparents are so excited about your book." She didn't know I had modeled the characters Nana Helen and Grandpa Jack after my own grandparents. Then she added, "They say, 'We're gonna be famous!'" That's absolutely something they'd say. I felt grateful they shared their happiness at my portrayal of them in my novel and also that I forgave and loved them for who they were in my life.

Call to Action

Who do you need to forgive? Is there a laundry list? Write these folks down, in order of your timeline of hurts. Who can you speak to in real time? Who can you write a letter to and never send? What would you say? What points would you cover? How could you end on a positive note? If you want to rise above negativity, start writing, and start making amends. When you make the decision to forgive, watch how your life begins to change. Believe.

49

ACT AS IF

Thoughts become things. If you'd like to feel more in control of your life, try channeling someone else, someone who you feel has life all figured out. Act like them, walk like them, dress like them—not in a carbon copy way, but in a way that allows you to emulate their energy and place you in the same vibration.

This exercise helps kids in activities such as sports and dance recitals and helps adults prior to public speaking and social events. For example, have your son or daughter channel their favorite player the next time they have a game, starting in the morning by having them think about what that person might be doing before a game, what they'd be eating, how they'd be thinking, what they'd likely be thinking while they brushed their teeth, and then have them carry that onto the field, court, or stage. I love that magical look on kids' faces when they come back to session and say the technique worked.

Are you about to speak at an event? Channel someone with confidence, a leader with poise, grace, and influence, especially if you don't feel that poise in yourself in the moment. Fun fact: I've even channeled a whale when I've been in session due to lack of sleep so that one half of me is getting zzzz's while the other half is giving the best I have to whomever I am working with, without wishing I was still in bed. William James said, "Act as if what you do makes a difference. It does."

PERSONAL SHARE

I've shared this story multiple times with my clients in sessions when we discuss manifestation. Back when I was pondering how to put my intuition and skills in personal development together, I didn't know how that would look or how to make things happen. My husband suggested that, on my birthday, a week or so later, I drive to a wellness center in town (I had met and admired the owner, who focused on holistic work in her counseling practice) and act like I worked there. My husband's idea intrigued me, even though I never thought I'd hear something like that coming from him (wasn't that *my* stuff??).

I did what he said. I drove there one morning, on my birthday over a decade ago, and I pulled into the empty parking lot, got out of the car with my cup of tea, and walked to the door like it was just another day at the office. Then I got back in my car, grateful no one was around to see me because I felt like an absolute weirdo. Fast forward a month or two later. Deena, the woman who owned the practice at the time, contacted me and asked me if I'd like to rent space. Well. Yes, I would, as a matter of fact. I've had my private practice in that office space ever since. BAM.

Call to Action

Who do you want to be? Who do you admire? Why? How could you emulate that person? When? What do you want to accomplish? Set goals to "act as if" the next time you have something important you'd like to achieve. Acting as if makes you feel better because you are acting like it's already happening in your life. What are you waiting for? Make things happen.

50

SMILE

"Your day will go the way the corners of your mouth turn." I love that quote, though I'm not sure whom to credit. Simple advice that works. Turn the corners of your mouth up. When you smile, you feel better. Your body follows suit and relaxes into happiness. When you smile, at least in that moment, you won't feel anxious or sad. Try smiling and see. Tara Brach often talks about smiling with the eyes and in the heart during her beautiful (free) meditations. Smile throughout your body and you will be well. Like when Will Farrell says in *Elf*, "Smiling's my favorite," make smiling your favorite.

Call to Action

How often do you smile (to others and to yourself)? If you asked a family member or friend, would they consider you someone who smiles fairly frequently? How does that make you feel? What do you want to do about that fact? It's your choice. It's your life. Decide that it is worth smiling.

SAY YES TO YOUR LIFE

Do you fight the moment? Do you say no before you say yes? Saying no to potential opportunities coming into your life is rooted in control and keeps you rigid, deflecting new energies that could move you toward what you want at a faster frequency. You can trust me because I happen to be a "No" person by nature. That's the way my brain works. I am an automatic no, so my brain can control every possible scenario and then when I can relax and know that I am safe to proceed, I consider a "yes." Exhausting to reprogram, let me tell you. Alas, it can be done, I am happy to report.

If you too are a "no" at first ask, what would life look like if you were to say yes more often? To resist the urge to put the automatic kibosh on whatever foreign comes your way? When you stand in the place of expecting the Universe to support your wants and needs, you become open to the more fluid guidance and opportunity coming your way. Trust. Ask, and ye shall receive, but you must stay open and be willing to say yes.

Call to Action

Are you a yes or no person? What do you say no to that might be worth saying yes? Do you trust your intuition? When has your intuition served you? Would you commit to saying yes to one thing this week or today to see where the answer might take you? Note how you feel afterwards. Compare this to how you might have felt if you had said no. Saying yes more often moves you past the wall with power and intention.

52

FLOOD YOURSELF

When you start to feel your vibration going lower, you need to call in the troops. Turn on motivational videos and inspirational podcasts, (think Esther Hicks on abundance, Les Brown on manifestation, Tony Robbins on personal development, Oprah on anything and, my favorite teacher of all time, especially when I need a good sit-down, Eckhart Tolle).

Find the people who make sense to you, wherever you're at on the path. Listen to the audios that motivate you, read books of inspiration, watch *The Secret* for the fiftieth time. We watch *The Secret* in our house pretty much every January. And after my husband's and children's big, "Noooo, we're watching *The Secret* again??" my family finds new insights each time. (Take what you need from the documentary and leave the rest behind.) Flood yourself. However you see fit. Yearly (not enough). Monthly, better. Weekly, even better. Daily, best. Gain lift-off on a regular basis to feel great.

Call to Action

When you need positive reinforcement, who are your people, both ones you know and those you don't? Make a list and keep it handy so that when you need inspiration, you can immediately turn to the list for lift-off. Be proactive and you'll find yourself being less reactive. Flood yourself to feel better. Start today.

53

HONOR YOUR SOUL CONTRACTS

This always constitutes one of the deeper discussions I have with clients. I believe you have soul contracts with the people closest to you in your life. For those relationships that challenge you and cause difficult feelings, whether mother/daughter, boyfriend/girlfriend, boss/employee or friend/friend, try to look past the illusion of the personality and attempt to connect on the level of the soul.

This perspective provides a more elevated view of relationships, when you can get past personalities and see what the other person's soul just might be here to teach you. I've had some incredibly painful dreams that have illustrated just how difficult it can be for the soul on the other end of the relationship to do what they have to do to us, too, in the name of helping us get to where we're supposed to go. As a result, I look at things differently, even when I'm confident the other person's ego might not be consciously aware of what they've done. Trust that people are in your life for a reason, to make you better, to help you rise in vibration, all in the name of contributing to the collective consciousness. Then, move forward in greater personal power.

Call to Action

Think back to the most difficult relationships in your life. What did you learn that at first seemed would break you (and maybe did in order to break you open)? What would you say to that soul now? How could you look past the difficult people in your life in order to see what their souls are offering you? How might that change things? You'll view hurtful situations in different terms when you honor relationships at this level. Believe.

54

EAT RIGHT

Food affects mood. Oh yes, it does. You are what you eat. If you eat junk, you'll think like junk. I think back to how I used to eat—living for Pepsi, bagels with cream cheese, and steak and cheese subs on an almost daily basis, oh, and as much sugar as possible, please. Think about how you feel after you eat certain foods. During the years I ate terribly, my thoughts were terrible. Then, when my husband bought me a stack of books for my twenty-seventh birthday, including *Beat Stress* by Leslie Kenton, I started to examine my foods and their effects upon my thoughts and emotions.

For example, if you want to feel more grounded, eat more protein. Watch your sugar. Sugar exacerbates anxious thoughts, similar to the way you feel when you're riding a bike down a steep hill with your feet off the pedals. Eat sugar at the right time—before exercise or when you need fuel (just not before studying if you tend to have a hard time focusing). When you do have sweets, enjoy every morsel. They're delicious! Don't deny yourself good food that's meant to be enjoyed. Be smart about the choices you make and know their effect on your body.

Me? I like dark chocolate. That's my fix in the afternoon hours. Chocolate raises dopamine naturally. (Thank you Daniel Amen, M.D.) I like carbs too, because they're good for my OCD brain.

I feel irritable without them. Too much, though, and I start to feel inflamed. Focus on balance. You generally need a protein, carb, and fat at each meal. Eat well to think well. Eat light and right. Most importantly, listen to your body.

In addition to feeling better, eating light and right sharpens your intuitive abilities. When my intuition came calling, during my first pregnancy, I knew I needed to eat more vegetarian foods after my son turned one. Eating light increased my clarity. I do eat meat now, though in moderation, but that works for my blood type. Trust your intuition when you're eating, and how you feel when you eat certain foods. When you get really good at listening, you'll know even before you touch something to your lips whether or not you should.

My body tells me when I'm about to enter inflammatory territory, little signs I've learned to listen to over the years—a grumbling in my belly, or a rushed, almost manic feeling even before I choose to eat food that contains sugar. This never fails me when I heed the warning. When I don't, I regret that lazy-ass decision. For example, I might yell at my kids after I've overeaten. Sound familiar? If you're a parent, has that ever happened to you? Annoying, right? Eat well to feel well. It's that simple.

Call to Action

How do you eat? What do you eat? How do you feel about an hour after you eat? Grounded? Mind racing? Start a food journal to track your moods around food. I keep a food log in my calendar every day to motivate me to stay on track. Do your own science experiment and see how you feel. A great read: Daniel Amen's *The Brain Warrior's Way*. The book offers helpful tips around eating to feel good. Track your meals, your snacks, and your moods for two weeks. See how you feel. Decide what stays in your daily menu. Decide what needs to go. Who else is going to decide those choices for you? Trust your intuition on what foods treat you right and move forward.

55

LEARN TO RESPOND VERSUS REACT

Jon Kabat-Zinn, Ph.D., in *Full Catastrophe Living* writes, "It takes practice to catch stress reactions as they are happening. But don't worry. If you are like most of us, you will have plenty of opportunities to practice."

Pause before you say or do something you don't mean. This one's not easy but well worth the effort. Don't you always wish you had hit the pause button after an ugly incident you might have initiated? Train your brain to switch from reactive mode to responsive mode. This creates a different charge. Once you choose to put the tool of responding versus reacting in your toolbox, you are much more easily able to eradicate anxiety. Responding helps you feel more in control.

If in mid-conversation with someone you feel triggered for any reason (the other person insults you off-handedly, insults someone you know, or disagrees with your personal values), squeeze your fists or toes to interrupt the flow of energy that's surging you toward reaction. Think before you speak. Decide how you want to present yourself and how you want to feel after the interaction. Angry or graceful? Edgy or classy? Pausing helps rewire impulsivity. This exercise takes practice. Eventually, though, you arrive at the point where your body naturally gives you a reminder, a little nudge to pause, so you can decide before you proceed.

Call to Action

How do you want to present yourself? Where do you feel triggered? When? With whom? How can you pause the next time you're in a trigger situation? How can you respond versus react? Responding is accompanied by a surge in personal power. Start responding versus reacting. What are you waiting for?

56

TREAT YOURSELF

In *Creating Affluence*, Deepak Chopra writes, "Think in terms of luxury." I'm not talking manic spending. Treating yourself means purchasing something for reasons none other than you're worthy and you're acting as if you're worthy. I love how Jen Sincero in *You Are a Badass* shares the story about the car she purchased, at a time when she didn't have the money. Sincero bought the Audi she wanted, versus the car that made financial sense. As a result of that bold decision, Sincero shared that prosperity flowed into her life in ways it hadn't previously. Inspiring.

When you think in terms of luxury, you set the law of attraction in motion, bringing to you the resources you need to make things happen. Note: treating yourself doesn't have to mean in big ways. Ordering organic food is a form of treating yourself, or choosing a more flavorful cup of coffee or tea, or like one of my clients did— buying a nicer wallet, one she felt matched better with who she was in the process of becoming.

These small acts of treating yourself help design a better landscape for your life. It's your canvas to paint, your story to write. Decide what that looks and feels like to you and move forward, through the wall.

How do you define luxury? What do you enjoy? On a grand scale? On a smaller scale? What could you do today to create luxury in your life, knowing you're worthy? Act as if and make it happen.

57

LISTEN TO MUSIC

Music can change your mood. While working out, driving long stretches, or creating a meal, listen to music you might not have heard in a while—loud. Music gets you high, the best kind of high other than meditation. Hard rock, hip-hop, classic rock, pop, country, whatever your genre. Go there, turn the music up loud, and visualize your goals coming true, while the energy is high.

Raise your vibration through music. Watch how your thoughts soar as a result. Sometimes I listen to music in my car, loud, before I see clients, and I end up having the kind of session you don't forget. Words stick, the message gets received. In those moments, I know it's not "me"—music simply elevated me to a place where I was able to deliver what I needed to, so my client could receive the message they required in that moment. Music can change your mind and your energy in an instant.

Call to Action

What kind of music sets the tone for you? What kind of music brings you down? Lifts you up? Helps you release emotions that have been stuck in your chest? Create time to escape through music, and see how you feel on the other end. Believe.

58

AVOID ALCOHOL

I know. I like red wine, too. Here's the thing: do you struggle with depression? Well, alcohol is a depressant. You know this already. You don't have to give it up altogether, unless you do—if you are one of these people, then you know in your heart that message speaks to you. Otherwise, be mindful. Drinking feels like a cure for social anxiety in the short term, yet that's the illusion. In the long term, drinking often causes those endless loops of OCD, depressive thoughts, and guilt, especially because when we drink we lower our inhibitions, so we tend to become more impulsive and reckless— precursors to those lower-vibration feelings. Drinking ultimately keeps you in a tug-of-war behavior pattern of "I feel good/I feel awful."

Be mindful of when, what, and how much you drink. Personally, I need to feel safe when I drink, with people I can trust. I like a glass or two of wine when out to dinner with my husband or with my cousins and close friends. That's about it. That's when I enjoy drinking most. Honestly, if I have more I get stupid, and that doesn't work for me anymore (thank God).

Here's my spiel I give to my adolescent clients: If you're a young person, try your best not to drink until your brain is done developing at twenty-five years old. Not twenty-one. Twenty-five. I know, I know, I was your age, too—and I wish I knew then what I know now. Try your best to hold off until then. Why mess with a good thing? For adults, moderation is key. Understand that the gremlins LOVE when we get drunk, and off the path, whispering in our ear, chug, chug, like we're still at some keg party in college. If you really want to feel better, are you okay with that? You get to decide. Remember, the choice is your own.

Call to Action

How often do you drink? With whom? How do you feel during and after? What do you wish you had done differently on the occasions you had too much? **Tip:** If you like to drink in social situations, try holding a wine glass or mug with your favorite soda or sparkling water. Sometimes just holding something in your hands for comfort helps you to feel social and like you belong. Most clients I've recommended this to report that this technique WORKS.

STOP SELF-MEDICATING —AVOID DRUGS

Rather than drugs, try supplements instead. I consider drugs to be a dark energy and a maladaptive escape. I'm not saying I'm against modern medicine when needed. I'm talking using drugs off the street to escape. Consider supplements to give you what you're looking for. I sometimes use GABA for reactivity, 5-HTP and Magnesium to help with relaxation and sleep and always a quality fish oil, like

Nordic Naturals. Supplements have done so much for my life, and while I am not an M.D., I get much of my information from great doctors like Christiane Northrop, Daniel Amen, Tieraona Low Dog, Deepak Chopra, Arlene Dijamco Botelho, and Andrew Weil.

In addition, I like Bach's Rescue Remedy for anxiety around exams and social situations, and homeopathic remedies for an overloaded brain at the end of the night, such as Silica. The list of alternative options is never-ending. Seek and search and find your own methods—without unpleasant side effects—to help you alleviate your distress. Then, if you've tried alternatives and they don't help, turn to medication. If you need medication, you take medication, that's my motto. Drugs without a prescription? Not so much. If you're serious about building stronger mental health, you'll avoid drugs. Trust your intuition.

Call to Action

What's your escape? Why? What specifically are you looking to avoid? Journal your symptoms. Can you research other means? Talk to a homeopath or naturopath for natural remedies, or peruse your local health food store. More people are becoming versed in these alternatives. Consider speaking to your doctor about your options. Know that you have choices. I'm a big fan of supplements and remedies and have done well using them for years.

60

LIST TWENTY-FIVE THINGS YOU WANT TO ACHIEVE IN YOUR LIFETIME

Grab your journal, or a fresh, white, lined piece of paper and write down twenty-five things that get you excited and inspired. This exercise should be playful and fun. The idea of a beach house, convertible, an English garden, connection with someone special, peace in your relationships and within yourself, the legacy you want to pass on to your children, whether that be a small fortune or an ideology of knowing that life is beautiful every single day and that just as we are, we are enough. Whatever you want to achieve, take time to list what's important to you and your life. What motivates you to want to succeed, moving past the gremlin voices of why you can't, why you won't? Instead, open yourself to why not?

Call to Action

Get your favorite cup of tea or coffee and make yourself comfortable. Create your list of twenty-five, then tuck it in your journal, pocket, bag, or briefcase, or stick it on your fridge, somewhere you can see the list or access it easily. View your twenty-five monthly, or view it daily. Check in with yourself on whether you are closer or further away from creating the life you want. Some things take planning. Pick one and prioritize that focus for the month, whether it's visualizing having attained what you want or taking actual steps. Big or small, it doesn't matter; that's how you arrive. Ask the Universe for guidance on how to make this one goal, or all goals on your list, manifest in your life. As you review your twenty-five, you may find yourself closer to some of your dreams than you think.

PART IV

TRUST YOUR INTUITION

61

TUNE IN—LEARN TO TRUST YOUR INTUITION

I taught my children to tune in at a young age. I had them close their eyes and "see" what their gut told them their next teacher would look like, or be like. I did this for their coaches, or upcoming situations, little science experiments they could conduct in order to compare results. Over time, my kids strengthened their intuitive muscles that they would need later to decide on friends, courses, roommates, parties. This exercise taught them to learn to trust themselves and their inner knowing. Your intuition never lies.

I love to hear my kids say now: "I'm getting a no on that" or "No, that doesn't feel right to me." This is a tool to start practicing at any age. You're never too old to learn. Trust your intuition, that inner navigation system that serves you above all else. The most powerful part of intuition, in my opinion, is that intuitive knowing requires no explanation.

When I get intuitive information on somebody or something in my life and I know I need to step back or take action, I don't feel the need to defend myself, the way I normally would if the information was simply coming from my personality brain. When I intuitively know, I know. Quietly. Privately. When you come to value your intuition, you grow stronger.

Call to Action

Close your eyes and take a few deep breaths. Center on a question you'd like the answer to. Keep things simple at first. More playful than life-altering. For example, what car should I buy? Or, what would be the best paint color in my bedroom? Then, see what comes. Did you get a yes? No? Good feeling? Weak feeling?

Sit for a moment, allowing specifics of your intuition to settle into your being. Then go about your day and see how the results compared to what you "thought." Try the exercises again, building up to more important questions: Is this the right doctor, medication, relationship, home, job? Record your results. Keep practicing. Like flexing your bicep muscles, you get the best results the more consistently you practice.

62

GET TO KNOW YOUR GUIDES

I mean the ones in Spirit (in the other realm). If I haven't already, I'm going to get a little out there in this segment. Do you believe you're watched over and guided? When you're at your lowest, do you believe deep down that someone's watching over you? I do.

If you're curious, start asking who guides you. What do they look like? What's their name? Is your guide an ancestor or an even higher form of being? No, really. Get past the weird. One of the greatest actions you'll ever take with regard to strengthening your mental health is connecting to Spirit in this manner. When you open to a higher plane, you'll never feel alone again. Ask your dreams, or ask during meditation, or a nap, to be shown your personal guide. Here's the essential part: trust what comes. Even some silly name that comes to mind, one you think can't possibly be the name of your guide. Keep the information personal and sacred. Because it is.

The guides that have been with me for years, on several subject matters, have never failed to provide the most pertinent, specific, beautiful information pertaining to whatever challenge, crisis, or question I am pondering. These relationships have been amazing, profound, and have never, ever failed me. I'd never go against guidance from Spirit. I acted on guidance to call detectives on cold cases in the early years of my work, risking my reputation—worrying I might look like a fool. Instead, I emerged pleasantly, incredibly surprised. You'll likely have several spiritual guides over the course of your life, similar to how you have teachers, coaches, and mentors across varying areas of interest. The difference is that you come to trust that your guides are always there, giving you a sense of power that previously, in the throes of depression and anxiety, you never thought possible.

The depression I dealt with in my early life—crippling, overwhelming, sucker-punching depression—doesn't come the same way anymore because of the guidance I've received. When I feel down, I feel my guides there all the while, standing on the periphery, waiting until I understand, however long that process takes. This makes for a very different life experience. Choose to connect with your guides, the highest guides available to you, so you're able to experience this type of relationship.

Call to Action

Have you ever felt guided? How? From whom? Your ancestors? Have you ever asked for help from someone or something? Who guides you and for what purpose? Would you like to connect with your higher guides, those in the spirit realm who watch over your life and offer information from a more evolved perspective? Ask. Ask to be connected with the highest form of guidance available to you. When the student is ready, the teacher appears.

63

CONSULT YOUR DREAMS

Look to your dreams when you don't know your next best move. One of my favorite exercises with clients is to have them consult their dreams. Ask a specific question you'd like the answer to and see what comes. Great wisdom lies in the subconscious: *information we already know and are simply waiting to uncover.*

When you come to value your dream guidance, anxiety and depression lose the hold they once had over you. Asking your dreams for information means you are learning to go within to find the answers you seek, creating powerful mental health. Caution: your gremlins do not like this exercise.

My favorite part of this strategy occurs when clients return to session after having done the homework. With bewildered looks on their faces, clients report that, lo and behold, after not dreaming for years (which to me is a sign you are blocked), they had a meaningful dream! Amazing what can happen when we ask for information.

PERSONAL SHARE

I can't tell you every situation where this technique has worked in my own life, but I'll choose one good example. When I started having some doozy dreams while pregnant with my first child, I realized I needed to do something with my intuition. I just didn't know what. I wasn't the type of person who wanted to hang a sign outside my door stating, Jill Sylvester, Clairvoyant (no offense to those who do—I went to them in the early days of my path and many were so insightful). That just wasn't my particular style.

That feeling of needing to use my intuition in some type of career grew stronger, yet I still didn't know what to do. So, being a dreamer, I asked. *Tell me the next best step to take.* That first night, I saw myself at Bridgewater State University, taking a master's class in counseling. I woke up stunned. First of all, my undergraduate degree was in business management and finance. Second, I thought I'd have to hightail it to Boston two nights a week to go back and get my second degree. I never considered a college twenty-five minutes from my house (on the back roads!), which allowed me to be closer to my children who were young at the time. That worked for the lifestyle. So that's exactly what I did.

My master's took me five years to complete, but I enjoyed the pace. After I completed my clinical work, I opened my practice as a licensed mental health counselor with a holistic bent, using my intuition in the form of reading energy as a supplemental tool during my sessions with clients. This career began from being guided by my dreams. I opened my mind to ideas I definitely wouldn't have had otherwise.

Call to Action

Write down your dream question at bedtime. Be specific. Example: Where should I go to college? How do I deal with my child? What does my child need from me? What is the next best step in order for me to start my own business? Be as specific as possible. Then put your journal or piece of paper by your bed. Allow the dreams to come. Ask for three consecutive days. When you wake, start writing. This only takes a few minutes. Sometimes you'll write pages. Even if you don't think it makes sense, write it down, for three days. Sometimes the answer comes the first night. It's fascinating what can happen when we open to that portal!

64

SET BOUNDARIES

This one's a biggie. Setting boundaries means deciding for yourself what feels right, what you will and will not tolerate, and what you will choose to do if you feel like your boundaries are being violated. Then you need to stick to your decision, and act on your word. When someone crosses your boundary line you feel infringed upon, sometimes literally, like when someone is talking too close to you or the person who keeps touching you when they talk. Also, when you are touched without giving your consent in a physically inappropriate relationship.

Emotional boundaries are crossed when someone speaks down to you, pushes their views on you, or tries to make you do something you don't want to do. For example, the person who insists on taking up more of your time when you stated you no longer wanted to discuss a certain subject. Honor yourself immediately when you feel your boundaries are being crossed. You'll feel this viscerally. It's an energetic loss of power.

I used to get awful stomachaches when my boundary lines were being crossed, by telling people more than I intuitively wanted to because I thought I should for their benefit, or worse, telling people what they wanted to hear just so I could end a conversation.

Whenever you feel this way, your body offers you an important message. Act on the information. Choose to be brave. Step back and allow the other person infringing on your well-being to be who they need to be, while creating a boundary line for yourself. What does this look like in real time? Take a spouse who constantly complains after a long commute from work. Allow that person to vent for five, maybe ten minutes of your time and then, hold your hand up, letting them know that you too have had a busy day. If you're a stay-at-home parent and your spouse feels that being home doesn't carry the same weight as being at work all day, yes, it does—you're running the business of your family, allowing your spouse to go out in the world with no worries.

You are in charge of your life and your space. You get to decide what feels awful and what doesn't belong in your own energy field. If people don't like this new and improved version of yourself, that's okay. They don't have to. They can go find someone else who wants to listen to their negativity. Decide what you want and then let people know by being solid in your own energy space. This action step creates true personal power.

Call to Action

From which people do you need to protect your space? When does your body let you know? How? What is important to you and what are you no longer willing to tolerate? What are you willing to do to set boundaries and protect your space? How does it feel when you make that choice to stay solid in who you are? Celebrate that choice.

65

ASK GOD, OR YOUR HIGHER POWER, TO BE YOUR AUTOPILOT

Not copilot. Autopilot. Some days we just don't have it. Running on empty with virtually nothing to spare. This becomes the time to ask God, the Universe, or your guides, to take the wheel. Let go and trust that someone, or something else, has your back. They do, just like the *Footprints* poem for those of you who are familiar.

The many times I've asked God to take over and steer, I've felt this sense of relief, similar to when you're really sick and aren't required to do anything. When you let go, be willing to let go. Fascinating how when you do, things move forward, often in the best way possible—problems solving themselves, new ideas presented, the momentum continuing, without your help. When you get out of your own way and let the Universe take charge, things usually work out even better.

Call to Action

Choose a day, an hour, where you ask for help, asking God to take over. Journal the results and see where things ended up. How did you feel letting go? Why did you let go? How did the day/hour turn out? What did this action step do for your faith? Trusting is a large part of good mental health, knowing in both our hearts and minds that everything is going to be okay, even if we let go a little.

CONSCIOUSLY ESCAPE

We all need to escape. The good kind of escape: quality TV shows, mindless TV shows, comedies, inspirational books, mysteries, fantasy fiction, music, exercise. Many of my clients say they get a lot of their ideas during long car rides or in a long, hot shower. Writing fiction, for me, is the great escape and always has been, since I was a young girl, writing stories for hours on end in my bedroom. Reading after a day of work and watching TV or a movie on Friday nights also helps me get out of my head. And I don't want to think about who I'd be without my morning runs.

Many people use alcohol and drugs as a way of self-medicating to escape their pain. There are other ways to escape without being self-destructive. Set your intention and make a plan to escape on a regular basis—the healthy kind. Establish a weekly or daily plan to get out of your head. You will be far more present and grounded when you return.

Call to Action

What is your current form of escape? Might there be a healthier alternative? How often can you plan to escape during the week to take a break from the routine of life and get out of your head? Plan. Schedule your escape. Enjoy your time when you're there.

67

YOU ARE WHO
YOUR FRIENDS ARE

Who are your friends? If you're surrounded by people who gossip, do drugs, lie, cheat, and steal, or are simply negative in their speech, chances are you may be too. Take inventory and think about who you are now and who you want to be. Do you surround yourself with people who make you feel the way you want to feel? Do you become "that" person yourself by being in certain company?

Choose your circle wisely. If you are working to feel better about your mental health, you need to spend time around those who already have this going on. When I think of my close friends, along with my clients, I smile. I know that by being around them—most of them, though not all—I feel better. My circle has the ability, just by being who they are, to make me feel good.

If you're around people who drain you, you want to take immediate action in this area. Make changes. This doesn't mean you ditch your friends altogether; simply tweak your schedule. Spend less time with those who bring you down, or represent an old, outdated time in your life, so that you're not continually discussing the past. Sometimes, though, you do need to say good-bye to certain people in your life. This takes courage, but ultimately brings you greater personal power and peace.

Call to Action

Who makes up your circle? Are you surrounding yourself with positive people or those who drain you? How do you feel when you're with your "friends"? If you're not with people who make you feel better or make you laugh or support your goals and dreams, who would you rather be with? Who might you take a step toward? What are you waiting for?

68

ASK THE UNIVERSE FOR CLUES AS TO WHY YOU'RE HERE

I have observed through the years that with every single person who comes to me with depressed-type symptoms, they simply aren't living their purpose. When you are doing what you are meant to, you simply don't feel depressed. When you live with purpose, the world presents as a different place. You look forward to getting up in the morning and beginning each day.

If you haven't figured out why you're here, or for what purpose—you have one, I assure you, we all do—formulate the question. Ask the

Universe to show you a sign, a clue as to the answer. Surrender to that answer and stay open. If you remain skeptical and dismiss this exercise as airy-fairy, you will miss the consistent guidance that flows in your life on a moment-to-moment basis.

Think back to when you were seven or eight years old. How did you imagine life would be for you as a grownup? What activities and role-playing games did you like to play? Mine was writing stories, talking to people, and playing the role of teacher in school. When I think of how I occupied my time then, and what I love doing now, I smile; it was right there all along, even if I veered off the path for awhile, reconnecting many years later with what I'm all about. I trust that that's what was supposed to happen.

Think back to your childhood and what activities you loved. Do your current activities relate? If not, ask for a sign. If you don't get one right away, that's okay too. Stay the course. Look for synchronicities like that right person who says the right thing at the right time, causing your mind to open to new ideas or nudging old ones that have been dormant. Be open to the answers you seek and follow the Yellow Brick Road.

Call to Action

What do you enjoy doing most? As a child, what did you think you'd do when you grew up? What did you love to do around seven or eight years old? Can you connect the dots? What's one thing you could do now to move you in the direction of aligning with your purpose? What on Earth are you waiting for?

69

INDULGE IN COMFORT FOOD
ONCE IN A WHILE

I'm all about the green smoothies—that's how I start my morning—but sometimes we need to indulge in comfort food as a way of making ourselves feel nurtured and cared for. Just like your grandmother, mother, or favorite restaurant makes. When feeling down, indulge in what brings you comfort. Two big bags of chips is not comfort food. You know what evokes good feelings when you think about true comfort. For me, it's homemade gluten-free pumpkin pancakes with maple syrup and whipped cream—it's also a cheeseburger and fries when that suits the mood.

On a particular night, day, or morning when you just can't get out of your own way, enjoy a warm meal—oatmeal with brown sugar or eggs and bacon, and sit down and enjoy every bite. Do not berate yourself while you're eating, "OMG, the calories. OMG, this is so bad for me." That is not enjoying the experience of indulging in comfort food. Say instead, "This food nurtures me, is perfect for my body right now, and I'm going to enjoy every single bite." Sometimes I even add, "This food makes me skinny," just for fun. It's all about intention.

Call to Action

What is your comfort food? When's the last time you enjoyed that meal? When can you plan to indulge and be good to yourself? Trust your intuition and know when and what you need. Then enjoy.

70

WORDS MATTER

In the words of Don Miguel Ruiz, "Be impeccable with your word." Think about what you want to say, really say, whether to someone next to you at the soccer field or your boss when you're asking for a raise. Three people come to my mind when I think of those who are thoughtful with their words. I notice this trait every time we converse. I admire this quality and aspire to be more like these three in this particular area. These thoughtful conversationalists are also consistent, not changing the way they speak in certain company. Side note: when they swear, the word is used as punctuation for emphasis.

People who are deliberate in their speech have more power and effect on others. As my mom used to say, which I've only come to appreciate now in my life, "Say what you mean and mean what you say." More words to live by. When you speak impeccably, you're true to who you really are. When you're true to who you really are, you feel powerful. Speak with intention. Trust that intuitive voice, that little whisper that knows what to say and what not to say. Move forward.

Call to Action

How do you speak? Gruffly? Negatively? Intelligently? Caringly? How do you wish you spoke in certain circumstances? Whom do you wish you were more like in speech? How will you channel this in your next interaction? How consistent are you? Watch how you speak today, noticing the tone and quality of the words you choose. Note how you feel as a result. Choosing to speak with intention creates a stronger energy. Trust your intuition on both what to say and what not to say. Feel the difference. Feel your personal power rise as a result.

71

CHANGE YOUR EMOTIONAL TEMPERATURE

When you're not feeling so hot—and of course that still happens even when you are doing this work—trust that feeling as soon as you catch it and change the degree of your emotional temperature. Run your hands under cold water, step outside in the cold air and breathe, or go outside and feel the warmth of the sun if you're inside in an air-conditioned room. This instantly brings you back into alignment.

My favorite way to change the rising emotional temperature of thoughts that no longer serve is to run a cold shower. This technique of choice is not as harsh as it might seem. You can start with a warm or hot shower, but then simply turn the temp down a notch, then do it again, then lower it again, until the water feels colder. You will immediately feel the film of negativity around your body drop like a sheet. Try it. My clients love this one. Standing under a cold shower helps you immediately feel stronger by bringing you back into the present moment. *You can feel the shift.*

Change the temperature of your emotions by creating a different sensation for yourself. Bust through that wall holding you back, keeping you in that stuck place. Create a different emotional charge and take control of your feelings. Taking control of your feelings helps you take control of your life. Trust the process.

Call to Action

The next time you feel an intense emotion, take a cold shower or run your hands under cold water. Notice how you feel. What was the intensity of the emotion before on a scale of one to ten? What is the feeling now? Put this tool in your tool bag to be taken out any time you need to balance the inflammation and intensity of your mood. Move through the wall. Move forward in your life. Trust.

72

NOTICE YOUR THOUGHTS

How you think is how you feel is how you behave. This is the root of Cognitive-Behavioral Therapy. If you think you're a born loser, you'll feel awful, causing you to behave in a maladaptive manner. However, if you change the initial thought to: *I am a winner surrounded by like-minded souls*, are you going to feel bad or better? Exactly.

Notice your thoughts and steer them where you want them to go. Take control of your mental health by being aware of how you think.

This practice is hugely important and worth the effort of coming to terms with how often you think negatively. When I started this awareness work, I was dumbfounded by how pretty much every other thought I had was negative or berating. I assumed I'd never be able to think positively. Well, I'm happy to write that I do—most of the time. You can absolutely retrain your neurotransmitters and the focused, dedicated work required to make those changes is worth every bit of effort. Do not give up on this practice. When you are committed to the work of becoming stronger, you will arrive on higher ground.

Call to Action

How often do you think positively? Negatively? What affirmation could you state to replace your negative thoughts? Connect the dots in your own life to how you think, feel, and behave. Make the choice to think in a more positive manner and move through the wall with gusto.

73

USE CONJUNCTION SENTENCES

Put things in perspective. For example, when you come home from a long day after an arduous commute, inclined to focus on what's negative, start with complaining (we all need to vent) but then add a conjunction sentence, which looks like this: I feel so tired and drained from the drive and my job after a long day BUT I feel so grateful to be home now for supper, to wind down, to be with my family. Or this: I am so nervous about getting up on stage and performing during this play AND I'm ridiculously excited about the idea of sharing my gifts and talents with the world.

Vent first but don't end on that note—add what is good. This type of thinking naturally redirects your negative brain. Add a conjunction word to your sentences. Own both the positive and the negative, the dark and light. A strong person is able to identify and work with both. Part of becoming stronger is first accepting what is and then finding the good in order to move you forward to a better feeling.

Call to Action

Write three situations you find difficult. Now write three conjunction sentences to those situations that you find challenging. Make them your mantras for when you feel down in the hole. See how you feel as a result of owning both the dark and the light. When you engage in this practice, know that you are emerging victorious in the area of powerful mental health.

74

NOTICE IF YOU FEEL MANIC

Pay attention when you're feeling you have to do something immediately or else you won't be okay—when you interrupt, cut people off, eat more than your share, or have to get to the door first. That surge of energy that almost feels desperate, overexcited, and takes you away from the present moment and out of yourself. Trust in your intuition and be honest with yourself when this is happening, in order to give your dysfunctional behavior greater meaning.

I realized at one point in my own personal development work that I would feel rushed inside myself, a slice of manic, when I felt excited about something. I'd eat fast, talk fast, and behave fast. I discovered that this experience often happened when I felt happy. When I sat with the feeling longer, I realized that happy was such a fleeting feeling for me for so many years, that subconsciously I would have a "Get-it-all-in-now-girl-cause-this-ain't-gonna-last" kind of feeling. And, well, that's not okay. Unacceptable, actually. I knew I had to change my undercurrent way of thinking to, "I am happy. I deserve to be happy. Happy comes often and I can relax into the feeling and expect more."

Over and over I repeated some derivative of this mantra. When I became aware of how nervous I felt when I experienced happiness, I could laugh at myself and change my thought pattern. I began to slow down when I ate, drank, drove, and connected with others, not wanting to rush the moment. I began to enjoy the feelings of happiness, knowing I deserved to feel those feelings and expect more.

Call to Action

How many feelings did you feel today? Can you identify at least three? Have you asked the people in your circle how they feel today to help them get in touch with their emotions? Practice proactively going through your day, taking inventory of how you feel so you can better understand and manage your emotions. Check in with yourself. Know how you feel, be honest and trust your intuition on claiming both the good and the bad feelings so you can notice the behavior that comes along with the feeling. Victor Frankel said, "Suffering ceases to be suffering at the moment it finds a meaning." Find the meaning. What are you waiting for?

DON'T STRESS IF YOU CAN'T SLEEP

If you *don't* get your sleep and you want to, don't stress. Trust that you're awake for a reason. Place your hand on your heart and breathe energy into your heart center to relax. Calm yourself. Get ideas; gain perspective. Grab your journal. Meditate. Some of the greatest ideas come from that quiet space.

During the night, or that lucid state right before awakening, you're most able to receive inspiration. Spirit can reach you in this space—when you can best process dreams, ideas, and messages that will serve you in your waking state. I find that 3:00 a.m. to 4:00 a.m. bears fruit. From midnight to 2:00 a.m., I'm more likely to hear the voice of gremlins. That's just my own code. I've learned when to go back to sleep and when to sit up and listen. After you get what you need, plan to get your appropriate amount of sleep the following night and be sure you establish good sleep hygiene to set yourself up for success (see #23).

Call to Action

What do you feel might be the reason you're not sleeping? What is that little whisper saying to you? Jot down ideas. Journal what you feel you need or want to do from those ideas. Decide action steps you can take now to move forward one step at a time. Note how you feel each time you make the choice to listen to your inner voice.

76

DO THE OPPOSITE OF WHAT YOUR GREMLINS TELL YOU TO DO—LISTEN TO THE OTHER VOICE

There's a reason I've dedicated three sections to the gremlins. They're nasty little buggers! Are you an oppositional type who doesn't like to be told what to do? If so, this technique will surely work for you. When the voice of your gremlins tells you to keep biting your nails or continue ruminating over something stupid you said last year, stop for a moment and tune into what the voice on the other side of your shoulder might say—the voice of your highest self, your angels, your guide. That voice might sound like this: "You know you don't have to keep doing that if you don't want to."

The next time you start explaining yourself to someone and your body cringes at the immediate awareness of the loss of power, stop mid-sentence and do the opposite: cease the conversation, step away and say you need to use the bathroom, take a pretend call on your phone. Do something different. Do the opposite of what your gremlins want you to do by thinking instead about what your highest self wants for you, what would feel so much better, if only we would dare.

Other examples: If your head hangs low while you're thinking thoughts that don't serve you, lift your head up. When you catch yourself thinking something negative, think of an opposing thought. Try smiling when you don't feel like it. If you don't like to be told what to do anyway, why are you doing what your gremlins are instructing you to do? These exercises may make you feel irritable at first. However, when you arrive at the understanding that there's always another way to look at situations, another way to think about your thoughts, you've come to trust the voice of your highest self. Then you can move through that wall of irritability with ease, experiencing the sensation of standing in an entirely new space, a space of emotional freedom.

Call to Action

What are you willing to do the next time your hear the command of your gremlins? What would the voice of your highest self say? Note how you feel as a result of this awareness. Turn up the volume of that other voice, that one that never forces you to do something, but instead offers you an entirely different, lighter perspective.

77

SET A TIME LIMIT TO VENT

We have a rule in my house. You can grumble and complain when you get home, but only for five minutes. Maybe ten or twenty should the problem be fresh off the press, but cap off your complaining. At a certain point, kvetching becomes counterproductive. Don't discuss your complaints again once you're done. Otherwise, you reinforce what you don't want.

Venting can be healthy; you need to release your emotions. When venting becomes habitual, though, particularly droning on about the same subject over and over, you need to set time limits—both for yourself and those around you. Releasing negative energy with intention is healthy and smart. Emotionally vomiting on everyone you come in contact with about your godawful life, just because, becomes toxic. You'll know you're doing this when everyone around you runs for the hills when they see you coming. Do you want to be known as that person?

Honor your time limit and move on. This way you set an intention for the venting, controlling the amount of yuck you're putting out in the world. Trust yourself when you've gone on too long, that little whisper reminding you that hyper-focusing on the negative really isn't what you said you wanted for yourself. There is tremendous power in letting things go.

Call to Action

How often do you vent? Are you a healthy venter or a toxic vampire? Who do you want to be? How might you limit your conversations with the intention of releasing and still keep the environment pure? Set your time limit for complaining. Move forward into a lighter space.

78

BALANCE YOUR LIFE

If you do too much of anything, whether that's work, socializing, or binge-watching TV, life can get out of balance. Think about where you spend most of your time and where you would like to insert other activities in the course of a day. Balancing your life creates better feelings.

You know intuitively what activities you over-do and cause you to feel stressed. If you work too hard or too much or at a job that doesn't make use of your gifts, make sure you get together with friends, get to the gym, or go for an outside run. Pay attention to where you feel out of control and think of one thing you can do to feel more at ease. When my kids were small, I asked my husband to finish his phone conversations for work while parked in the garage so that when he entered the house, he brought a different energy to the space.

What's one thing you can do to bring things in balance in your life? Balance doesn't mean perfection. When you choose to do one thing different in order to bring balance to your life, you're far more present with others during the moments of your day, which means you won't miss them. Remember John Lennon's quote: "Life is what happens to you while you're busy making other plans." Yeah, it's like that. Choose balance. Feel better.

Call to Action

Think about where and how you spend most of your time. Could things be better? Where could you be more balanced? Where do you feel intuitively you might be missing out? What are you willing to do to bring about change in this area? What are you waiting for?

79

IMAGINE SOMETHING DIFFERENT FOR YOURSELF TO CREATE A DIFFERENT FEELING

Use your imagination. This will perhaps come to be the most important tool in your tool bag if you truly want to change your life. It's become the most important tool in mine. Einstein said, "Imagination is more important than knowledge. For knowledge is limited, whereas imagination embraces the entire world, stimulating progress, giving birth to evolution." Imagination evokes change by dreaming of what could be. The mind makes no distinction between what is real and what isn't. If you see it in your mind, it is.

PERSONAL SHARE

I could give endless examples of using my imagination in my own life. For time and space, I'll share two. First, when five years old, imagination became my lifeline, my safe space. Still is. I used to visualize a tree house in my backyard, so much so that that tree house, with its dark floor boards and braided, multicolored rug, exists as real in my mind now as it existed then. Yet it wasn't even there. I didn't have a tree house. I simply wanted one. I went there nightly before bed, daily during my frequent day dreaming, picturing that cozy, dark space, feeling protected and welcome. That tree house played an important part in my childhood, even though it didn't exist on the physical plane. Another example, is when I got hit by a car and broke my knee at the age of twenty-nine. I nearly went out of my mind on the first day when I realized I would be unable to work out or move for months. I had entered panic mode, my body not generally liking that kind of forced rest. As a result, every day, I closed my eyes and went on my runs. I did my loops. I felt the feeling of being outside in December, that cold fresh air making me feel recharged. I did this faithfully over the course of two months. And I never gained a pound, or felt out of shape when I fully recovered. I felt fit and mentally well, stronger actually. I imagined those workouts and felt the sensation of running, my mind unable to distinguish between what was real and what was not.

Imagination is programming what you want to happen, feeding that vision, and then reaping the benefits by feeling good. Create that safe space in your mind, create that dream job, that relationship you crave, that outcome you desire, and feel the feelings while you're imagining. Take time to imagine every day. See how your life unfolds as a result. Believe and feel great.

Call to Action

Where is your safe space? What is your picture of achievement, of success, of happiness? Take time nightly, before bed, and go there in your mind. Play. This is how manifestation works: easy, effortless, and playful. Those are the delicious ingredients of imagination. Do this nightly. Fall asleep to your vision. You will come to crave this sacred time, where you nurture your personal ideas and dreams.

80

PRACTICE YOGA

Another game changer. Whether done in class, a retreat for a week, or in your home alone, you will never regret practicing yoga—a practice for both men and women—although I must admit, yoga might challenge you at first. If you want to feel better, take a class and stick to this routine weekly at a minimum.

Yoga grounds, evokes mindfulness, and creates beautiful metaphors for life, such as holding poses when you're shaky, allowing your vulnerability to surface while emerging on the other side unscathed. There are many types of yoga. Try what feels best to you—whether Hatha, which is more gentle, or a rigorous form of Vinyasa in a heated room. There are also many good videos online you can follow to perhaps begin in the privacy of your own home. Work through the poses, all the way to Shavasana, or corpse pose, allowing the practice you've done to work for you in this final resting pose.

PERSONAL SHARE

When I started on the holistic path, after my husband gave me the slim, little book *Beat Stress* by Leslie Kenton—a book that has become a tiny treasure in my life and sits on my office shelf—I became intrigued by the idea of yoga. My intrigue likely having to do with the fact that my sixth grade teacher told me I was such a nervous wreck I'd have a heart attack by the age of thirty. So! I took a yoga class at my local gym, where I did cardio classes. And . . . I hated it. Like, really hated it. Like, I kind of wanted to give everyone dirty looks (and might have). Everyone seemed all relaxed and chill when I wasn't.

The opposite of chill, I felt annoyed at how I wasn't moving and that I wasn't sweating, like I did in my beloved cardio classes. *This is so stupid*, I said to myself, *I'm not doing anything productive, damn it*. I went home that night and complained to my husband about how awful the class was. Then I felt annoyed by that, because I had said I wanted to try yoga so badly. Something inside of me made me try again, that "energy of the bees," that whisper of my highest self, never forcing, simply encouraging, a voice saying, *maybe just one more time.*

This time, at the end of class, during the meditation part, I had my first out-of-body experience. My whole body shook as if I was having a seizure, except that I wasn't. I lay there, still, but I could feel my body vibrating visibly. The person next to me looked over, noticing too. I left that class forever changed. Something had awakened in me. An experience I couldn't explain, but I knew something had happened to me and that I was different, that things were going to be different.

I had embarked on a new path without realizing I stepped off the old one. I can't promise this will happen for you in the same way, but I can tell you, if you trust that little whisper, you will attract new things into your life, aligning with the path the Universe has in store for you.

Call to Action

Have you ever tried yoga? What prevents you from starting? Try different variations—perhaps a different class each week or month to see what resonates with you. Research different classes for homework and schedule them in your calendar. Keep going until you feel a fit. Stay with the practice. Yoga may take a few times. Trust that you'll connect with your body in a way you never have before. Enjoy the practice.

PART V
FEEL BETTER

81

DO FOR OTHERS

In *How To Stop Worrying and Start Living,* one of my favorite books in the whole wide world, Dale Carnegie wrote, "Try to think every day how you can please someone." A powerful remedy for stronger mental health: get out of yourself. You can always find someone who can use a kind word, an act only you can provide, or a simple hug for encouragement. Sometimes just asking someone, "How can I help?" can release that person's stress on the spot. Whenever I'm in my head, mad at someone, or upset about a situation, I go to work with my people and immediately I get out of my own stuff and into someone else's story. This creates perspective in your life and gets you out of your own drama. You tend to emerge with a softer sense of things, in a state of grace.

Volunteering also works wonders, whether with animals, people, or outside quietly working with your hands. Do for others and think about helping someone else. When you do, you inadvertently help yourself. Time goes by and you find you're not thinking about you, your life, your issues, your negative stuff. If you want to feel better, if you want to finally feel stronger in the area of mental health, you will focus on other people and what you might be able to do for their life to help them in some way, in addition to focusing on your self.

Call to Action

When was the last time you did something for someone just because? Listened to them? Helped by offering a task or spending time, offering your expertise or helping with chores? How did you feel before, during, and after the task? What did this act do for someone else? What did this do for you? When is the next time you could do something for someone else? Who needs your help, either in terms of time, tasks, or talk? Schedule it in your weekly plan and make it happen. Feel better as a result.

82

SURROUND YOURSELF WITH BEAUTY

Look up and all around you. Beauty presents everywhere: flowers in the garden, foliage in autumn, soul in your dog's eyes. When you're not feeling aligned, create your own version of beautiful. One of my mother's best traits is her ability to make any surroundings homey and nice—whether an apartment in the city or a modest home in the suburbs.

Rise above doom and gloom by decorating your environment with simple, beautiful things. Whatever that means to you—a garden, a stack of new books, beeswax candles, or a clean tub that invites you in once a week to soak and rejuvenate—surround yourself with what makes you feel good. Make a practice of surrounding yourself with simple pleasures: manicuring your yard, early morning fishing watching steam rising off the water, sitting by the ocean, listening to the sounds of the waves crashing against the sand. Notice how you feel when you keep things simple, when you focus on pleasure instead of pain, and when you become aware of the creative power you possess to surround yourself with beautiful.

Call to Action

What does beauty mean to you? If you could surround yourself with beauty, what would that look like? What one thing could you do today to arrange your work or living space so that it feels better and more inviting? Put something nice in your space that you can see every day to remind you of the beauty blossoming in your life.

83

GET OUT OF VICTIM MODE

This is a process I believe we all must go through in order to rise up out of the ashes, so to speak, to become who we are truly meant to be. Think the Hero's Journey. You have to know darkness to know the light. If, for example, you've ever been made fun of as a child, it's highly likely you have become more empathetic because of that trauma. That horrible experience may have assisted you in transforming those awful feelings into something good, by developing compassion for others. Another example: if you've ever been left out of a group, or not been invited to a gathering, I bet you make a conscious effort to include others when you can.

Don't blame your past—thank your past. It's when you stay stuck in the experience, complaining about the same thing over and over, that the event becomes counterproductive. There is a time and a place for being a victim. And there's no right or wrong length of time. After all, your journey is your own. However, you may want to become aware of how long you've been hanging out in victimhood so you can move away and rise up into that higher space that awaits you as a result of understanding that sacred wound.

You will know when victim mode has gone on too long from the social cues: people don't want to listen to you anymore; they move away from your space with a polite smile (or not). You become "that" person. I spent many years in victim mode and that vibration became a driving factor in my decision to become a therapist. Decide for yourself when it's time to open the door and free yourself from victim prison. Remember, you have a choice.

Call to Action

How do you notice when you might be playing the role of victim? When have you felt like a victim in the past? How many times? With whom? Is there a pattern? Are you ready to break free of that pattern and create a different dynamic for yourself? How might you find yourself in victim mode in your present life, saying statements like, "I'm always broke," versus speaking in successful ways, such as, "I'm on my way to abundance." Catch yourself when you step into victim mode and immediately decide to change the verbiage or behavior so you can feel better.

84

STOP SETTLING

Lift yourself higher by behaving in ways that show the Universe you deserve, and desire, more of what's good in life. If you like good food but consistently buy yourself cheaper versions, stop that behavior pattern. Buy what you prefer. You can save money on other things. Stop settling for what you don't really want and make a conscious decision to move toward what you do want. This also applies to relationships.

I have listened to female clients over the years say they wish they had different people in their community. Different women to walk, run, or play tennis with—rather than friends who consistently complain about the same topics or continually gossip about other friends, which makes them feel worse, not better, after a forty-five-minute walk in nature meant to nurture the soul. "I have no one else to go with," these women say. Or, "There's no one else out there," my male and female clients say when they're settling for relationships that are sometimes emotionally and verbally abusive. Really?

How about exercising or spending a Saturday night by yourself—shutting one door with confidence, trusting another will open, surprising you with a more aligned person to share your time and space with. Stop settling for conversations and friendships and relationships you don't want to have. Do like Shonda Rhimes instructs in *Year of Yes* and say, "No, I'm not able to do that" when someone asks you to go somewhere you don't really want to go or do something you don't really in your heart of hearts want to do. Open to something else by saying no to what you are no longer willing to settle for. Be brave. What comes after you take the leap toward feeling better often feels great.

Call to Action

Where do you settle? In what area? With whom? If you were a more confident person, what three things would you no longer settle for? Decide right now that you're going to act like a more confident person and execute your plan. Act as if. Then watch what happens. Observe and enjoy what the Universe mirrors back to you when you make the choice to no longer settle for less than you deserve. What are you waiting for, 'cause the Universe is waiting on you.

85

STOP SPEAKING NEGATIVELY

Avoid negative speak: talking down about yourself, about others, about life in general. If you are a person who speaks negatively about yourself, your job, your relationship, your woe-is-me life, take inventory. Do you feel better or worse when you engage in negative speak? Are you someone people would describe as positive to be around or are you the Eeyore in your group? When was the last time you initiated an inspiring, uplifting conversation? Pay attention to what you bring to the table.

Take gossip, for example. Look, I'm an emotionally intelligent person. I know if you're talking to me about someone else, you're talking to someone else about me. Stop being that person. Develop a no-gossip zone with your friends out at dinner, or at home, instead discussing topics of value or just plain nonsense and fun.

Of course, there are times to tell stories; that's what confidantes are for, but deep down, you know the difference. There's a seedy vibration to speaking negatively, polluting the air with your mal intent. And if you're being honest with yourself, when you diss on someone else, you're really trying to feel better about yourself in front of other people. Confident people don't talk down about another person or themselves—they like their own personhood just fine and value what other, positive information they bring to their relationships.

Choose to be a more confident version of yourself: talk in positive ways about your life, your job, what lessons you might be learning, where you need to improve, inspiring others to do the same. Talk positively about other people, recognizing the good your friends, your co-workers, your neighbors are doing, and the success they are having. See how that behavior makes you feel. Talk positively about the world: trust that we are right where we are supposed to be, to learn the lessons we need to as a collective consciousness and that when each one of us does our own good, psychological and spiritual work, we raise the vibration of the planet.

Stop speaking negatively. Immediately feel better.

PERSONAL SHARE

I was at a ball field once, stuck between two women, one of whom had a tendency to yap about other people. After the "yeah, yeah," response, hoping the conversation would naturally end on its own, I challenged myself and stepped back. Literally. Out of the negative energy dynamic. For a second, things felt awkward for the person because I believe she realized what I was doing. Then, immediately, as if sent from Heaven, a good friend of mine walked past at exactly the right time and we began chatting, smoothing the moment right over. That's how the Universe works when you make changes for the positive: in your favor.

Call to Action

When do you tend to be negative? With whom? If you're really being honest, why? What are you willing to do differently the next time you're sharing space with these types of people? How can you transform negative behavior in your home or work space, ultimately contributing to the good of the collective conscious? How would you feel if you made those changes?

SET YOUR INTENTION

Life is all about intention. Your strong mental health depends on your conscious intention. Before you do anything, from beginning chores around the house to driving to pick up your kids, set your intention of how you want that next part of your day to go. Jerry and Esther Hicks call this segment shifting, one of my favorite takeaways from the book, *Ask and It Is Given.* You gain greater control of a situation by stating beforehand what you want from the situation. By understanding how you want to feel, you learn to direct your mind on how you want things to go, versus going through the day putting out fires, allowing the sections of your day to own you.

The more you practice setting your intention, the more you flow with life. For example, set intentions such as, "I drive safely and enjoyably to work," "I speak with ease during this party and connect with like-minded souls," "I work easily and effortlessly today, feeling productive at the end of my work shift," "I am happy, content, and worthy." Watch how the parts of your day go when you consciously engage in this behavior pattern. Compare how you start a segment to how you finish when you set your intention. Setting intentions single-handedly helps develop powerful mental health.

Call to Action

Write three intentions for your day today. State them out loud or in your mind before you begin an activity or interact with someone. Notice how you feel after the activity. Practice this new technique throughout the day. Check in with yourself as to how you feel. Feeling better? Thought so.

87

EVERY DAY, CONNECT TO SOMETHING GREATER THAN YOURSELF

Look at the sky, the sun, the sunrise, the sunset. Stare until you feel small, in the best, most humbling sort of way. Notice the beauty, the power in these spiritual experiences that put our little lives in perspective. When you sit in a spiritual space, whatever that looks like for you—nature, church, temple, meditation or prayer in your bedroom—ask yourself, is it really all about me or is it about the role I play in the world in order to serve the greater whole?

Connect to the Source of all things, to God, the Universe, whatever you believe, and feel the harmony and alignment within yourself when you say that prayer, stepping out of your solo viewpoint and into the blueprint of us all. Darkness all but dissolves when we connect to something greater than ourselves, for we experience the power of what truly makes the world go round.

Call to Action

What is your spiritual practice? How often do you practice connecting with something bigger than you? How often would you like to connect? Once a day? Three times a week? What would it look like if you chose to include this exercise and connect with Spirit every day? Connecting takes only a few minutes when we set our intention. Do you think you might feel better? What are you waiting for? Marvel in existence.

88

TAKE AN AFTERNOON BREAK

Everyone does better with a break. Breaks allow you to hit the pause button and take inventory, deciding if you would like to feel differently than the way you do at the moment. My body has become so used to taking an afternoon break that I grow sleepy every day between the hours of 1:00 p.m. and 2:00 p.m. For you, taking a break might mean stopping for a coffee and sitting in a coffee shop, taking time that you deserve.

Every afternoon, stop and check in with yourself as to how your day is going, noticing what might feel off and unimportant. Think about what you'd rather be doing, and also reflect on what feels right and forward flowing. Give yourself permission to take time just to dream about something other than a task at hand. This is how you plant seeds for change. New ideas are born from daydreaming.

Taking breaks helps manage your emotions so they don't get the better of you, to step back off the crazy train you might often find yourself on, not realizing you're the only one who can stop the momentum. When you tune into your emotions and take the time to realize you can choose to do something differently, you get a far better handle on depression- and anxiety-related symptoms. I taught my kids at an early age to take breaks. We called this quiet time. Evvvvvverybody needs quiet time.

I've stuck with my practice of quiet time pretty much every single day since in order to step back from the demands of life and take inventory. Most days, my quiet time lasts twenty minutes. Longer on Fridays. Taking breaks isn't selfish. When you take a timeout, you're better to the people around you. We're talking simply twenty minutes for a catnap, reading, or whatever activity resonates with you. The intention of a break is to stop the madness and refill your cup. As a result, you have more fuel for the remainder of the day. Besides, when you take mental breaks, your gremlins are far better behaved.

Call to Action

What time could you stop every day to reflect on where you are? What time would you need— fifteen, twenty minutes, maybe an hour one day a week? Sometimes all we need is five minutes to stop and reflect, and then realign with where we'd like to be. Maybe you could take a break in between projects or tasks, or if you're a student, in between subjects so as not to become overwhelmed. What do you think a break would do for you? Note how you feel when you do versus when you don't. Schedule a break in your day today. No excuses. You're working hard on your mental health and taking a break is part of the process.

GET BACK INTO YOUR FEET

When my kids were little, most nights we'd do this activity: we'd twist back and forth in our bare feet to root down into the rug before bath, before bed, to bring all the "crazy" energy from the day back down into the Earth where it belongs. This worked like a charm and helped us wind down for sleep.

I still sometimes do this at night when I get ready for bed, twisting the energy of the day into the ground, allowing me to feel more balanced. I'm a sensory sort of person, so the exercise feels good to me physically, causing me to feel connected, rooted, and safe. When you are doing a lot of work on yourself, you often find yourself in your head. When you do, simply make the choice to get back into your feet, allowing the work to do what it's truly meant to do—help you feel better, more balanced, and more peaceful in your body.

Call to Action

Each day, morning or night, ground your feet— bare feet are best, though not required—into the Earth. Twist back and forth until you gain more strength and feeling in your legs. Or sit in a comfortable chair and press your feet into the floor while you breathe. In the morning, visualize the Earth giving you all you need to move through the day with ease. At night, visualize letting go of all the excess energy you've absorbed from the day. Feel those good feelings and celebrate the work you are doing by consciously making yourself feel better as opposed to looking outside yourself for the answers.

90

TAKE SOCIAL MEDIA BREAKS

Yes, even if you're not a teenager. Take breaks from everyone else's happy, perfect, beautiful lives. Trust me, as a therapist, I can tell you that's likely not the whole picture. Feeling down often comes from comparing yourself to everyone else. If you start to feel bad from surfing online—or your body sends you a migraine—shut down the connection. Use technology for what you need. Social media can be an amazing tool. However, when you're done researching for work or pleasure, shut the thing off and go read a book, go for a run, or even better—go talk to someone in person.

Use social media for good and recognize when the beast sucks your energy and you become unproductive. Like anything else, moderation is the best practice. I remember posting a picture on Instagram one Sunday morning of my perfectly set dining room table with a post that stated how everyone was home for breakfast and our family time together was going to be great. The table looked so inviting! Meanwhile, shortly after I posted, my son stayed in bed because he felt tired (from playing Fortnite) and I sat at the breakfast table feeling sad because the four of us weren't sitting together like I planned. So much for the post! The picture looked great, but that's not really how things went down.

Call to Action

How often do you engage in social media? What do you enjoy most? What don't you enjoy? What do you need technology for? What time limit per day, per subject, would be healthy for you? How do you know when things become unhealthy? What are the signs your body gives you? They're there. Trust those messages. Power down for periods of time when you're at home. The information will still be there the following day. Make the choice to honor how you feel.

91

REMEMBER THE MOMENT

My husband used to say this a lot when we'd be somewhere as a family, say a hike in the woods, in order for us to recall the details of the memory. Like taking a mental picture of a moment in time. It's about standing in the power of now, grasping a piece of where you are and what you are doing, and tucking that memory into your heart so you can unfold the detail at a future date in order to feel the same feelings. Stand in the moment and think about what you'd like to remember. Part of becoming aware is realizing that you'll never stand in this point in time again. Choose to enjoy where you are and make your moments good.

Call to Action

How often do you remember the moment? What moments do you remember most? With negative moments, consider how they might have played a role in your life, propelling you to where you are now. If you aren't where you'd like to be, how might you create new moments now that you'd want to look back on in the future? The moments of now shape your future. Make them good. Even a simple walk in nature can set the path for new memories to cherish. The next time you are somewhere and think, "Wow, this is wonderful," use the phrase "Remember the Moment" to store the memory in your heart. Instantly, feel good.

92

COMPLIMENT SOMEONE

Acknowledging the good in someone else, highlighting positive attributes in another person, allows you to feel better. Compliment someone, even when you don't feel like doing so. Find something good about someone else, like the way they fix things you can't or the way they find humor in situations when you tend to be overly serious.

You might compliment the way your mother or father makes a bed, folds sheets, or washes dishes, even though they might not be there for your emotional needs. Take the time to acknowledge others, all the while strengthening those neurotransmitters in finding what's right versus what's wrong. This technique instantly elevates your mood and contributes to your quest of obtaining more powerful mental health.

Call to Action

When was the last time you complimented someone? Why? What compelled you to speak? How did you feel after you gave the compliment? How do you feel when someone compliments you? Do unto others. Feel great.

93

KNOW YOUR STRENGTHS AND CHALLENGES

I typically begin work with clients using this activity to lay the groundwork for personal development. List your strengths— preferably twenty-five. Traits like: I'm a good friend; I'm a good listener; I draw well; I play the piano with skill; I make great meatballs. Stretch yourself and write as many as you can. Next, write no more than three to five challenges. Challenges such as: I tend to be an energy drainer; I turn to alcohol for my escape; I tend to isolate.

A mentally strong person knows the good in themselves in addition to their weaknesses. Sometimes a client will say to me that acknowledging strengths makes them feel like they're boasting. You're not boasting when you own your unique gifts. In contrast, you're embracing your personal power. Your gifts are what you are here to share. Who are you to withhold those gifts from the world?

I tell some of my clients: by the time we're done working together you're going to say with strength and purpose all the things about yourself that are fabulous and beneficial to the rest of us. At the same time, you will take personal responsibility for the areas in which you need to grow. That's the point of being a human being, isn't it, to learn and grow? That's what I believe. Listen, I don't want to have to come back and learn the same s**# again. All set, thanks. But that's just my philosophy.

Own your strengths and your challenges. Embrace both the dark and the light. Become whole.

Call to Action

List your twenty-five strengths. List no more than five challenges. Read your list daily, before bed or to start the day. Know yourself. Own who you are and who you want to become. Move forward. Feel better.

94

NAME THE BEST AND WORST PARTS OF YOUR DAY

Take the time to ask yourself this every day. If you have a family, this activity helps you connect, informing you where your kids or partner might be emotionally and what you might need to do to help. If you don't have a family, consider calling a friend or relative nightly and making this a ten-minute ritual. It's important to check in with yourself, and with your significant others, to identify what went well and what didn't, because each day presents both—you have good parts and not-so-good parts in a twenty-four-hour period, and that's normal and healthy.

Highlighting the negative and positive helps you accept both parts and not be so ruled by either in the long run. This activity builds powerful mental health. Journal or discuss the highs and lows daily in your own life, and in the lives of those you care about, because now you are teaching others how to avoid the consequential highs and lows of your emotions. Part of becoming stronger is being able to weed through the negative and to emerge unscathed, role modeling for others how to feel better. Share your good fortune. Feeling better is the feeling of abundance. What you put out comes back to you. Share your newfound wealth.

Call to Action

List the worst parts of your day first and then the best parts, always ending on what you're grateful for. Do this daily as a way to end your day. Check in with your emotions. After you identify both, how do you feel as a result? Check in on the emotions of those you care about. Help them to own their feelings by embracing both the best and worst parts of their day. Then, move forward in stronger mental health.

95

PAY IT FORWARD

Share what you know. Share what works for you with other people who might be struggling. When you feel better—and you will when you stay consistent in your practice—move that fresh energy out into the world. Be kind in your new emotional freedom; drive someone somewhere; make a donation to a new business that could use your support; pay for the person's coffee in the car behind you at a local drive-through; tell someone that everything is going to be okay, the magical, transformative phrase that we all need to hear several times along the path. Paying it forward is good karma. Paying it forward allows you to feel immediate benefits.

Call to Action

Decide today what you can do to send good energy out in the world. Share what works for you. Share your abundance. Feel great.

96

FOCUS ON TODAY

What if today was your last day on Earth? I don't mean that to sound scary. I ask the question to empower you. To live like today was your last. Would you worry then about how much sleep you didn't get last night? Would you stress about what someone said to you five years ago? Would you be kinder to your family members and your friends? Would you pay attention to the little things and notice every beautiful detail of every single moment of your day?

Focus on today, as if today were your last. Decide who you want to be and what you would want people to say about you if today truly was your last day on Earth. Live today with gusto. Break your day down into segments, making morning, afternoon, and evening even more special by being hyper-focused on that part of your day. Bring a better vibe to your work, your play, your interactions and exchanges—from the cashier at the drive-through window to your parents.

This twenty-four-hour period is all you are responsible for—not tomorrow, not six months from now—that will be a new twenty-four-hour period. Focus only on today and see whether you feel more empowered, more approachable, and genuinely happier as a result of keeping this singular focus. Decide how you want to live today, this twenty-four-hour period, knowing that the present moment is really the only amount of time you are responsible for shaping.

Call to Action

What would you want to accomplish if you simply had these twenty-four hours to live? What time would you get up? Who would you connect with? Where would you go? How would you bring yourself to your workspace, your family space, your moments alone? Write down how you would want people to describe you. What would you want them to know about you? Have you shared enough of your gifts? How might you start sharing those gifts today? Choose to be present. Feel amazing.

97

AVOID ENERGY DRAINERS

You need to keep your distance from energy suckers in order to stay sane. You can still love from afar. Here's an energy exercise I give to clients dealing with a difficult person in their home or work environment. In the presence of someone who threatens your emotional wellbeing, immediately shield yourself. Surround the person in an imaginary box, igloo, telephone booth, bubble, or whatever image works for you. I promise you, this tool works wonders. You can put your own bubble around you, too, keeping yourself self protected and cocooned.

Feel the protection of that shield, and watch how the telephone booth around the other person forces them to keep their energy all to themselves. Notice how the previously annoying, potentially damaging person who threatened to attack you no longer possesses that power. The best part is that the other person's pain body, as Eckhart Tolle references in *The Power of Now*, has no where else to land, often causing the person to seek healthier ways of dealing with their dysfunction. That's the best way to deal with—and help—energy drainers in your life. This technique never ceases to amaze me. Stay in your own lane so you can do your own important work. Remember, your good work affects the blueprint of us all.

Call to Action

Who drains you? Why? Is there a topic you need to address to come to a place of peace or is the issue the person's energy in general? How often do you have to be in this person's presence? Be smart. Can you limit communication to email or text? Don't feel guilty about this decision. Protect yourself and your energy as you work to create powerful mental health. Allow the other person to take responsibility for their own work. Role model how it's done. Inspire other people to reach higher. Feel purposeful.

98

EMBRACE WHAT IS

When you come to accept the power of the present moment, you offer less resistance, less fight, and less denying of your current circumstances; you can then move more quickly to the next moment, further away from what you don't want. A mantra or affirmation like the infamous, "It is what it is," helps anchor you in the moment of not-so-much in order to move more quickly to, "Yup, this feels much better."

When you fight the moment, yell, kick, and scream about how things aren't fair, and complain about why this happening to you, you delay the more relaxed feeling of acceptance. Accepting what happens immediately strengthens you, raises your personal power, your maturity level, and your evolution. Know that even the times in your life that were difficult were part of the journey to get you to right here, at this point on the path, where you are now able to open to a different state of mind. Choose to be present and enjoy what is happening. In the present moment, you have everything you need to be happy. Think about that.

What might you be fighting? What feels unfair? What mantra can you state for acceptance, the intention of which is to embrace the present moment? Once you've stated your mantra, what one thing can you do next to move away from the feeling you don't want with grace and understanding, in order to move toward what you do? Do that. Feel powerful.

99

STOP TAKING EVERYTHING SO SERIOUSLY

Be gentle with yourself. We can be so focused on our practice, on our growth, that our intensity becomes like an addiction. Are your spiritual practices like an addiction? Step out of the vibe for a moment. Where have you become rigid? How did you used to have fun? When was the last time you laughed? Do you have the ability to laugh at yourself?

People want to be around a person who can be both serious in their pursuit of happiness while relaxed at the same time. Use wonder and imagination to replace hyper-focus or addiction to goals. Take a breath and relax into right where you are, trusting that you are right where you are supposed to be.

Call to Action

Where might you be too serious? Do people consider you fun? How do you like to have fun? Who do you have fun with? Who are you serious with? Are you able to be fun and serious with the same people? Make a list of where you tend to be rigid and intense and decide where and how intensity can work for you beautifully and where it doesn't. Where are you willing to make a change? What is one thing you can do today, this week, this year to become more relaxed and at ease in your personal development practice? Do that one thing. Feel lighter.

100

VALUE YOUR STORY

We all have our stories, the good, the bad, the shame, the sacred. You are here to create, to share your story, to share yourself in ways you see fit. If you haven't figured out how to do that yet, you will. For starters, go outside and look up— everything is happening naturally, on time, in a rhythm that works without our frenzied efforts. Work hard, yes. Work very hard toward what you want. Then surrender.

Maybe your story has yet to be told. Trust that your chapters are unfolding exactly the way your story needs to, so that you can uniquely share and serve. This, I believe, is why we go through the things we do.

Call to Action

Share your story. Decide what that looks like to you. Trust your intuition. Move forward in the sharing. Feel better about who you are and about the life you have been given in the vein of service to us all.

I hope you have enjoyed these tips and will incorporate many of them in your own daily practice. I'd love to hear how you are learning to listen to your intuition and using the techniques.

Contact me by visiting my website

www.JillSylvester.com.

ACKNOWLEDGEMENTS

To my husband Carl for being the best editor I could have asked for (who knew?), Lisa Tener for developmental editing, Rebecca McCarthy, editor for my fiction books whose guidance influences everything I do as a writer, Jody Amato for copyedits, Clarisa Marcee for final proofread, Janica Smith for publishing assistance, Elena Gwynne for indexing, and PearCreative.ca for book cover and interior layout design.

To my beta readers: Carl, Laurie, Tracy and Michael Bailey, thank you for your feedback and for encouraging me to write more of the Personal Shares when I wasn't sure I wanted to include them in the first place.

To the many resources listed in this book, and the many not listed, who have contributed to my personal and professional work. Your work, your stories, inspire the rest of us in the area of authentic wellness and stronger mental health.

Thank you to my initial sample group of clients, cousins, family and friends who chimed in on the early considerations for the book's title. And especially to one male, former client in particular (you know who you are): Your heartfelt feedback on the humane aspect of intuition with regard to a book on mental health greatly influenced my choosing the final title.

To my children, Kyle and Michelle: your emotional strength, intuitive skills and the way you live your life in general, inspire me on a daily basis. If you have learned a few things from me in the area of mental health, particularly how to trust that wise voice within, well, that's the kind of legacy I'd like to leave behind.

Lastly, and always, to my clients, thank you for trusting me as your therapist. I hold that responsibility close, a treasure tucked inside my heart.

For more information about Jill Sylvester or to contact Jill for speaking events, please visit www.jillsylvester.com

RESOURCES
IN ORDER OF APPEARANCE

Harriet Lerner, Ph.D., *Fear and Other Uninvited Guests*

Norman Doidge, M.D., *The Brain that Changes Itself*

Andrew Weil, M.D., *Spontaneous Healing*

Mel Robbins—melrobbins.com

Tony Robbins—www.tonyrobbins.com

T.D. Jakes—www.tdjakes.org

Lisa Nichols—www.motivatingthemasses.com

Eric Thomas—www.etinspires.com

Jocko Willink—www.jockopodcast.com

Rachel Hollis—www.msrachelhollis.com

Joe Rogan—www.joerogan.com

Martha Beck, *Finding Your Own North Star*

Louise Hay—www.hayhouse.com

William Glasser, *Counseling with Choice Theory*

Marie Kondo—www.konmari.com

Paolo Coelho, *The Alchemist*

Julia Cameron, *The Artist's Way*

Deepak Chopra—deepakchopra.com

Oprah Winfrey—www.oprah.com

William Glasser, *Warning: Psychiatry Can Be Hazardous to Your Mental Health*

C.C. Chapman, *Amazing Things Will Happen*

Norman Cousins, *Anatomy of An Illness*

Planting the Seeds products—jillsylvester.com

Marie Kondo, *The Magic of Tidying Up*

Laurie McAnaugh—lauriemcanaugh.com

Wayne Dyer, *Your Erroneous Zones*

Jill Sylvester, *Land of Blue*

Tara Brach—www.tarabrach.com

Esther Hicks—www.abraham-hicks.com

Eckhart Tolle—www.eckharttollenow.com

The Secret documentary

Leslie Kenton, *Beat Stress*

Daniel Amen, *The Brain Warrior's Way*

Jon-Kabat Zinn, Ph.D., *Full Catastrophe Living*

Deepak Chopra, *Creating Affluence*

Jen Sincero, *You Are a Badass*

Christiane Northrop—www.drnorthrop.com

Supplements—see Daniel Amen's *Change Your Brain, Change Your Life*

Daniel Amen—www.danielamenmd.com

Tieraona Low Dog—www.drlowdog.com

Arlene Dijamco Botelho—www.allworldshealth.com

Andrew Weil—www.drweil.com

Deepak Chopra—www.deepakchopra.com

Nordic Naturals—www.nordicnaturals.com

Bach's Rescue Remedy—www.bachflower.com

Don Miguel Ruiz—www.miguelruiz.com

Dale Carnegie, *How To Stop Worrying and Start Living*

Shonda Rhimes, *Year of Yes*

Jerry and Esther Hicks, *Ask and It Is Given*

INDEX

O

ABOUT THE AUTHOR

Photography by Tracy Colucci

Jill Sylvester is a licensed mental health counselor who works with adults and children in private practice. She's based in the suburbs outside Boston, Massachusetts where she lives with her husband Carl, children Kyle and Michelle, and an adorable, mischievous bulldog named Jackson. *Trust Your Intuition: 100 Ways to Transform Anxiety and Depression for Stronger Mental Health* is her first non-fiction book.

To contact Jill, visit her website at <u>jillsylvester.com</u>.

f fb.com/jill.sylvester.771

⊙ @jill_sylvester

✦ @jillsylvester1

ALSO BY JILL SYLVESTER

Land of Blue

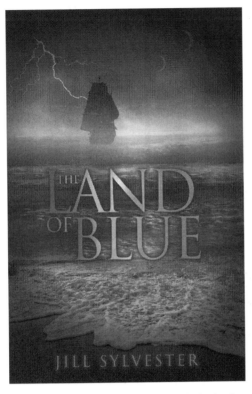

A young adult novel (for both kids and adults!) that takes readers on a fantastical voyage filled with hidden meaning, metaphors and messages, arriving at the destination of greater social and emotional well-being.

A wonderful tool for parents to read alongside their younger children.

The Land of Blue makes for powerful, thought-provoking discussion for middle and high-schoolers in both English and Wellness classrooms.

ALSO BY JILL SYLVESTER

Awakening

A Young Adult mystery series, *Devon: Dream Agent,* features seventeen-year-old Devon, a girl who uses her newfound intuitive gifts to work on solving crimes. Coming soon!

To learn more about these books visit
www.JillSylvester.com/books.

PRODUCTS BY JILL SYLVESTER

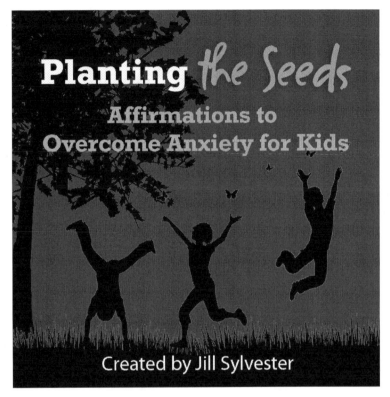

Affirmation Cards for Kids ages 8-12 / Caregivers may use these cards as a tool to help children develop emotional awareness, affirm individual strengths and ultimately overcome anxious feelings. Great for adults too!

PRODUCTS BY JILL SYLVESTER

Positive Energy Cards for Kids ages 5-8. Our set of 24 creatively illustrated Positive Energy Cards are a self-esteem building tool designed to encourage meaningful conversation between kids and their caregivers.

COMING SOON:
Planting the Seeds Cards for Adults

To learn more about these cards visit
www.JillSylvester.com/products.